GENERATIONAL INSIGHTS

GENERATIONAL INSIGHTS

PRACTICAL SOLUTIONS FOR UNDERSTANDING AND
ENGAGING A GENERATIONALLY DISCONNECTED WORKFORCE

CAM MARSTON

Jacket Design: Mark Johnson www.hiremarkjohnson.com
Layout Design: theBook Designers www.bookdesigners.com

ISBN: 978-1-4507-2443-2

Generational Insights
PO Box 81118,
Mobile, AL 36689
(251)479-1990.

Printed in the United States.

DEDICATION

This book is dedicated to the many managers, supervisors, team leaders, and employees who have tirelessly told me their workplace stories and have helped me understand what is working out there and why.

Also, to my children: Ivey, Mackey, Spencer, and Reiney — I hope you give employers fits some day, too. That will mean you're normal.

Most importantly, though, this book is dedicated to my wife, Lisa, who allows me to pursue this odd job of mine with the passion and zeal I need to do it justice while she keeps everything straight back at the ranch. She's the glue.

ACKNOWLEDGEMENTS

TWO PEOPLE helped complete this book and many times had to fight my busy calendar and lack of focus to do it. This book exists in spite of me, not because of me.

Acknowledgements must begin with Steven James who manages and leads my research efforts to find the data and information I need to support and enhance my claims. There is hardly a fact or figure out there that Steven can't track down that provides some much needed perspective.

Megan Merchant has been the most valuable contributor in this entire process. I shared with her my idea and she ran with it. She organized the information, arranged the interviews, checked the facts, and pushed me when I needed pushing. She has always been a treat to work with and this was no exception. Prompt, professional and just plain awesome. *Megan, thank you very much.*

CONTENTS

PREFACE

30 HOURS ON THE RIVER

CAPTAIN TED EWING *is a towboat captain. He has pushed freight up and down the inland waterways of the United States for thirty years. Ted began working on a towboat when he was in high school, working weekends and holidays on the Mobile River under the watchful eye of a veteran captain who told Ted that as long as his report cards showed good grades, he'd be allowed to work on the boat. So whenever report cards came out, Ted would dutifully show them to his parents and then bring them to his captain to secure a place on the river.*

Today, Captain Ted, as he's mostly known, leads the M/V FR Bigelow on the Lower Mississippi River between Venice, Louisiana, and Vicksburg, Mississippi – the most hazardous and busy stretch of inland waterway in the United States. He's responsible for a 7200-horsepower, $8 million vessel owned by Ingram Barge Company of Nashville, Tennessee, as well as cargo worth hundreds of millions in the 35 barges tied to his boat, and the lives of 10 crew who put themselves into Captain Ted's and each other's hands for 28 days at a time. The crew members work six-hour shifts for 28 days and then get 28 days off to go home, be with family, and get ready for the next stretch of time on the river.

The boat, when fully loaded with cargo and headed upriver, goes about two or three miles per hour against the current. Time can move slowly and the work is hard – particularly for the deckhands who, regardless of the weather, must be out on the tow checking straps to make sure that all is safe and that the barges won't separate, wreaking havoc on river traffic. The crew works in teams, and after working together for a while they learn one another's movements, understand each other's tone of voice. They work together in the blazing hot sun of summer and the cold sleet of winter, always on the water, out in the open. Frequent breaks to cool down or warm up help, but the work is hard, very hard. And Captain Ted is in charge of keeping everyone safe, working, moving forward, and, most importantly, wanting to return to work after the 28 days on shore.

As you might guess, such hard work followed by a month away can create turnover challenges. Sometimes the deckhands find it easier to not return to the Bigelow rather than work like that again. But Captain Ted has managed to beat the odds. His first mate and master chief have both been with him for years. And that's just the top of the list. Captain Ted has lower-than-average turnover, leaving him with a good, hard-working crew that is loyal to his leadership and wants to help him succeed. He has been through none of my seminars and he has not read my books, but he knows what is going on with the workforce and how employees are changing.

In January 2009, I was invited aboard the Bigelow as a guest of Ingram Barge. The company asked me to give several seminars to their captains and pilots to teach them about the changing workforce. Before I could begin the seminars I needed to see their work and working environment firsthand. So for about 30 hours I rode upriver with Captain Ted and his crew, boarding in Venice and leaving in LaPlace, Louisiana. I had never met any of them before and was a stranger to their tight-knit ship family, so everyone was on his best behavior. Soon Captain Ted and I developed an easy conversation and I learned a lot from listening to him. That night, as we were passing New Orleans, we started chatting and he shared what he'd figured out after years of working with the different generations of crew members:

"You can't hold someone responsible for something they've never been taught."

It was as simple as that. I had witnessed a moment earlier in the day, which clearly illustrated this philosophy. A new deckhand was with the crew on this trip. He'd never "decked" before and was learning the job the same way generations of other deckhands had learned the job – by apprenticing to someone with experience and by making a lot of mistakes. "Casey" was not afraid of hard work, but no one was quite sure if he'd make it, if he would fit in with the crew.

The morning of my chat with Captain Ted, the Bigelow had pulled over to the side of the river to set up a big tow for an upriver run. The process involved lining the first string of barges up perfectly straight so that the remaining barges could be tied to this straight line and everything would be ready to go. Getting that first string of barges straight is precision work requiring lots of pushing and pulling from the Bigelow and adjustments and help from smaller tow boats sent to help out. There were deckhands moving about, constantly calling to one another and to their captains for adjustments, working hard to get the barges lined up right the first time. It was taking a long time and the crew was growing impatient.

Captain Ted watched from above in the wheelhouse as Casey laid a strap between two barges. Captain Ted saw something about the way Casey laid that strap that he didn't like and called down to Casey on the radio, "Casey?"

Casey called back, "What?"

Everyone froze. They looked at Casey and then up at the big glass windshield of the wheelhouse where Captain Ted was watching everything on his boat and on his tow. Captain Ted paused a beat, maybe two, and then came back on the radio. "I need you to redo that strap, laying it the opposite way if you would. I think it will hold better the other way."

"Okay," Casey replied, and began redoing his work.

Why did this brief interchange stand out? The maritime industry is one of the most unique in the workplace today. Very strong rules and rituals still prevail where, in most other industries, time and change have forced old rituals to disappear. One of the maritime standards still strictly enforced is the way one addresses a vessel's captain; it is *always* "captain" or "sir" or ma'am." *Never* "What?" Hence the stares when Casey gave his direct, and unknowingly disrespectful, reply. Captain Ted talked about it in more detail that evening in the wheelhouse.

"You can't hold someone accountable to what they've never been taught. Casey is probably like most kids these days. He probably grew up with both parents working. Just as likely he grew up with one parent absent due to divorce. His mother didn't discipline him the way my parents disciplined me. She was too tired after a long day's work and the last thing she wanted to do was have a confrontation with her son. She knew her son needed discipline and hoped the schools would handle it for her. But, as you know, the schools don't want to discipline. They think discipline should happen at home, which, frankly, it should. But the result is that Casey probably has never been disciplined in his life the way I was.

"Then he shows up here to our workplace, where for 28 days straight, every six hours, you're working side by side with a well-seasoned crew who knows each other's very thoughts and you're on the outside. You don't even know

what questions to ask. On top of that you have the deep ritual and tradition of the maritime industry that is completely foreign to this kid who may have never even been on a boat before. Casey is so out of his element that he's hardly aware of what he doesn't know.

"In the past, when I was Casey's age, if I had said "what?" to my captain, he would have pulled the boat to the shore, wherever we were, and told me to get my belongings and get off his boat, that he wouldn't tolerate that type of disrespect. You could do that then. Today, you can't. And furthermore, it is so hard to find good people who know how to work that I'd be a fool to dump him off. Truth be told, he's never been taught discipline or respect. His mother didn't do it. His schools didn't do it. And I shouldn't have to do it. But I will. He can't be held accountable for something he's never been taught. So I'll teach him. And then I'll hold him accountable for it.

"Tomorrow morning when his shift is over, I'll catch him in the galley after breakfast and pull him aside and have a polite talk with him. I'll tell him what I saw him doing this morning that was very good work. Then I'll tell him about how he's to address me in the future. It will not be a disciplinary type of conversation, just an education. I'll explain to him something he didn't know and ask him to now be accountable for a new behavior. He'll need to accept these rules of how to address the captain or he simply won't work out here on my boat. I'll also ask his crewmates to reinforce what I've said to him. I think once he notices his crewmates addressing the captain appropriately, he'll quickly understand what he needs to do."

In my 30 hours aboard the Bigelow I began to understand just how unique management aboard a towboat is. In a normal workplace, an employee works eight hours, give or take, then leaves his coworkers for 16 hours before seeing them again. Aboard a towboat you have nowhere to go. You can't leave your coworkers. You can close the door to your quarters but if you want to eat, there they are; if you want to go outside for some fresh air, there they are. There is nowhere to hide, which makes management aboard a towboat a management pressure cooker. And those who have figured it out, as proven by low turnover and a strong safety record, tend to know a good bit about people and what makes them tick. And what I learned from many of the other captains I met with at Ingram Barge is exactly what Captain Ted taught me as we slowly pushed upstream past New Orleans:

- There are rules that simply must be followed ...
- And no one can expect to know the rules if they've never been taught.
- Teach them well and then hold them accountable for what you've taught them. This means you need to be a good teacher.
- Expecting someone to live and behave by the same unwritten code as you did when you "were a kid his age" is fruitless. Too much has changed and you're wasting your time.
- Show respect.
- Have patience.
- And if you've done everything you can and it still isn't working out, cut bait. No reason to waste any more time on a losing proposition.

The fundamental business need of captaining a towboat hasn't changed through the years. But how good captains approach today's crew members to get them aligned with the necessary procedures and goals most definitely has. As Captain Ted shared, it may not be the way he likes it, but it is the way it is. Figuring out how to adjust to the change is critical to success.

This book is full of stories of people who have figured it out. They have stumbled upon some ideas that have worked to make their workforce a better functioning unit. They have tried new things, worked hard to effectively teach people the right way, and have cut bait when it didn't work. The common theme is that they were having trouble and took it upon themselves to figure out the problem and solve it. In the process, they've uncovered some very effective, and often nontraditional, methods of managing, motivating, and retaining people.

My hope for you is that you can take some of these ideas as printed and use them in your workplace. Or take the nugget of the idea and create a different application of it for your workplace. The bottom line is that you need to do something different. If you're reading this, it is because something is not working right and you need to make a change. Do something. Try something. The old and true definition of insanity: Doing the same things over and over again and expecting different results.

Here's to taking a different approach.

Cam Marston
June 9, 2009
Ritz Carlton Hotel, San Francisco (Wishing I were in the wheelhouse with Captain Ted on the Lower Miss)

SIGN OF THE TIMES

When I started work on this book, the national news was focused on how long this recession would last. The debate was over whether this was a big one or a little one, and whether a stimulus package from the federal government would shorten the recession at all. The workforce was holding on, bracing for an impact, yet unsure exactly what that impact would be. Workers were hunkering down, watching the news, and speculating on how this economic crisis would impact them, if at all.

A year later as my team and I put the final touches on and send this book to press, we have a better view of how the economy is shaping up. What was once a speculation about an upcoming economic collapse has become known today as the Great Recession. Unemployment is hovering around 10 percent nationwide, and there is very little good news on the horizon as the government's stimulus package has done little to prevent the recession and many indicators suggest we will struggle in this economic climate for a while to come. *The workforce environment, mysteriously, remains largely unchanged.* The same issues that plagued workplaces prior to the recession are the same ones I'm getting requests about today. Companies large and small are still looking for resolution around four key areas: engagement, motivation, retention, and recruiting. Many are predicting a surge in job turnover when the economy recovers – Gen Xers and the Millennials will likely look for new employment that is either more challenging or more suitable to their lifestyle. And top talent, regardless of the economic climate, often has its choice of work. So even though the economy is on the rocks, the same people issues I studied during the heady days of a soaring economy are still the ones challenging workplaces, employers, and managers today. How do we work together despite a growing generational divide?

Bottom line: This content is still very relevant today.

CHAPTER ONE

WHAT'S ALL THE FUSS

And Why Do I Need to Fix Anything?

MANAGER OR MEDIATOR?

DAVID HOUCHINS was midway through the presentation at his weekly team meeting when the tension became evident. The cause? Texting (or IMing or Twittering).

The seven youngest members of his MassMutual Strategic Financial Group sales team, all Millennials, were clustered on one side of the table messaging each other, and who knows who else, about who knows what—probably what they'd done over the weekend or had planned for after work that day. The remaining team members, Boomers and Gen Xers, were only half-listening to the presentation, distracted by flying thumbs and seething on Houchins' behalf. Even though they stayed silent, Houchins could read his older team members' thoughts and was likely dead-on in his assessment of what they would be muttering under their breath. The Millennials were blissfully unaware of the ire cast their way. The meeting, and the team, was at a generational crossroads and Houchins found himself in the unintentional role of traffic cop. Could Houchins ease the tension and return focus to the work at hand? We'll find out in a bit.

This same scene is being played out in offices across the country. Whether it is texting at the table or time off to attend a school play, the desires and expectations of the different generations are making an impact on the way individuals work and how we work together. Even President Obama is changing the work environment at the country's most respected office by not wearing the traditional coat and tie in the Oval Office at all times. Is this disrespect or simply a more relaxed approach? As Houchins witnessed, different generations have different perspectives. Obama, a young Boomer on the cusp of Generation X, is setting a new tone at the White House; it seems that loosening the tie and rolling up the shirtsleeves is no longer considered anti-establishment. If the Oval Office can adapt, so can we.

A BRIEF HISTORY OF TRYING

DURING THE PAST 10-15 years, businesses have been adjusting to the impact of Generation X employees in the workforce. A much smaller generation than the Boomers before them, Xers entered the working world at a time of great advancement. There was a lot of growth in the late 90s and few able bodies to fuel it. As a result, Xers had some power despite their small numbers. Combine this talent gap with changing generational values and we had a business world in flux. Change was needed – the question was who should change?

Today, the Millennial generation has joined the workplace in full force – and there are plenty of them. Yet again, generational norms and expectations have businesses wondering exactly how to adapt. There is one critical difference this time around: Today, we understand that businesses need to do most of the adapting – now the question is what works.

The new work force dynamic is that of a blended family – everyone brings their own baggage to the table and it is up to the leaders to set the tone for how they can best work together. As with families, we often turn to those around us to see what mistakes we can avoid and what strategies we can emulate.

Throughout my 15-plus years of researching generational differences and consulting with business leaders about how to understand the strengths and challenges that each generation brings to the table, I have been privileged to become acquainted with several individuals and companies that seem to have it pretty well figured out. They've adapted to the changing workplace dynamic but maintained their fundamental organizational and managerial integrity. They are attracting the right kinds of employees and have the measures in place to both engage and retain them. This book shares their stories.

A STEADY COURSE OF CHANGE

WITH THE UPHEAVAL in the financial markets, government bailouts, and mass layoffs in almost all business sectors, you may be tempted to think that adapting to employee needs is a thing of the past. However, the truth is that each generation is still different at its core. Their collective history is an unchangeable piece of their DNA. Many employee perks have disappeared with constricting budgets; however the underlying values that created the desire for those perks remain within your employees. This is why it is still critical to look closely and adapt as necessary. Employees certainly need to adjust expectations, but businesses also need to remember that the drivers of those expectations are well-ingrained in each employee and will resurface eventually in some shape or form. Or as philosopher Simone de Beauvoir so bluntly observed, "In the face of an obstacle which is impossible to overcome, stubbornness is stupid." Generational mismatches are not going anywhere. To reach the desired result for your team and your business, leaders must be willing to adjust course to accommodate the changing current.

In times of prosperity, businesses and individuals have the luxury of testing the waters while finding the recruiting techniques, employee incentives and management styles that bring results. That wiggle room is missing now. You know you need to make changes and you want to know exactly what to do so that you don't waste time, money or energy. You want concrete examples of how to engage your employees so that they are more effective, efficient and eager to help your company succeed in a challenging market. That's what I'm here to discuss.

This book provides insight into:
- The different, and often disparate, ways generations view the workplace and why that still matters;

• The challenges associated with Gen Xers as they enter new life stages – both as parents and as managers;

• The risk associated with the retirement of Boomer leaders who will take both their institutional wisdom and classic team-driven work ethics with them;

• The challenges associated with Millennial workers as they leave prescribed worlds of home and college and move into a business world that is not designed specifically for them; and

• Strategic initiatives and simple tactics that leading companies and forward-thinking managers are already using to overcome these challenges.

With this knowledge you will be better prepared to match employee desires with company demands, helping create a workplace where all members are engaged and moving together toward a common goal.

FROM WHERE I SIT: MANAGER A, 47

THE FOLLOWING are comments from an interview with a frustrated 47-year-old Boomer who is working with a wide range of generations at a regional division of an international technology company. Identifying details have been omitted to protect both the guilty and the innocent, and because Manager A, while real, can easily represent any number of leaders in today's business world. He is why I wrote this book. Perhaps you've felt this same way at times.

On Exasperating Habits of Young Employees:
"Kids" have a tendency to confuse being busy with being productive – they get sidetracked by adding more/doing new things, and not necessarily delivering what was asked in the time frame that was directed ... a lot of "work" is taking place, but the requested product isn't getting out the door. How is that helping me achieve the company's goals?

They view deadlines as a recommendation and can get confrontational about timelines/restrictions – time may be a currency, but it needs to go both ways ... Millennials need to honor their agreements. 8:10 is not 8:00, and while it may not seem like a big deal, they have agreed to be in at 8. If I agree to pay $1,000/week and start paying them $998, you can be sure they'd complain about that difference.

It is especially frustrating when they assume time independence without following the procedures to get it – all they need to do is ask. In 15 years as a team leader I cannot think of one time where I have refused a request for time off. Just be respectful and show the courtesy of asking first – do not take it for granted.

They challenge everything. There is no understanding or assumption that the management team does, indeed, know what it is doing and that therefore when you are asked to complete something, you should just do it. They always question why. It is distrustful and defiant.

On Staying Employed in a Tough Economy:

Times are tough, so we told everyone they need to make themselves more valuable to the organization. Six weeks later, everyone on the team is taking that message to heart – except the Millennials. They seem to be content where they are and not worried about giving more.

Strangely, there are many Millennials who are clearly unhappy and not really with the program, yet they aren't taking any steps to leave either. Seems like a bad case of inertia. Seems like they want their hands held, but that's not my job.

I'm not sure what to do because my current "carrot" is clearly not motivating everyone to the full extent.

I'm looking for those who don't need handholding. I don't have time or desire to be a mentor. If you need help with your self-esteem, do that on your own time.

On Successful Millennials:

We have one 30-year old kid who is respected throughout the organization. He is in charge of people 10-15 years his senior, but because of his incredible work ethic no one questions him. We know where he stands and that he is committed. His leadership role is his reward for a strong work ethic.

Those who succeed still have a Boomeresque work ethic, even if they have youthful social needs.

The good Millennial is tech savvy, social, but very work-focused.

Expectations are in line with standing/experience and he knows he needs to work hard to get rewards.

Does anyone else see how Manager A could benefit from a sit-down with Captain Ted? Since a boarding pass on the Bigelow is hard to come by, let's hope he can put some of this book's takeaway techniques to practice.

WHAT'S WRONG WITH THESE KIDS ANYWAY?

THAT'S THE underlying question isn't it? Managers and business leaders who have moved through the traditional business hierarchy are often frustrated by the perceived lack of work ethic and high expectations of the younger generations. We've all heard the laments – Xers are not team players; Millennials need to be coddled beyond reason; there is a definitive lack of respect for authority and tradition; nobody is willing to pay their dues; etc. My interview with Manager A illustrates the feelings of so many business leaders today. You question why they can't follow the same path you did and just accept the way things are. You wonder when they are going to grow up and realize how "real life" works. While these are fair questions, they are not the right questions and dwelling on them does not ease the frustration.

Many of these complaints are grounded in truth. However, when you dig deeper and understand the whys behind the attitudes, it is easier to see how a rippled surface clouds a strong, hard-working current below. Much of what drives us crazy about Xers and Millennials is what makes them incredibly hard-working and fiercely loyal employees … *if* you make the connection and participate in their game of give-and-take. And let's face it: Hardworking, loyal employees are the foundation of any solid company so it is well worth the time and energy required to figure out how to meet your employees where they are instead of expecting them to come to you.

Too often we take for granted that others think the way we do. Yet time and again we are proven wrong. In fact, much of what the Millennial and Gen X employees desire in a workforce is counterintuitive to that which many Boomers, and certainly most Matures, equate with a positive work environment. This makes determining what to do and how to go about it quite difficult. It is our inclination to presume that these generational differences are simply a factor of youth – they will grow out of it and get with the program. Not likely. As Captain Ted acknowledged, they cannot be held accountable for what they don't know. And each generation simply does not act on the same foundation of experiences and expectations.

Understanding *why* the generations act differently is the key to success. When we understand what has shaped their perspective we can see that they still have values and they still strive for success. However, it is the definitions that change. Success, reward, value, time, commitment, loyalty – these all mean vastly different things from generation to generation. And the truth is that these changing definitions are having a strong and lasting impact on the employer-employee relationship. You simply do not want the same result, nor do you share the same values. This is not a fad, it is a business trend, and smart businesses must adapt to trends in order to stay relevant in today's market.

WAIT IT OUT OR WORK IT OUT?

AS I'VE GIVEN presentations to hundreds of organizations and businesses throughout the years, invariably an attendee asks, "Isn't this just a function of youth?" Yes and no. Much of the shift in generational work ethics and values, while most evident in youth, is central to the very being of each generation. Or to make it more personal, did you act like this when you were just starting out? Likely the answer is no. The 20- and 30-something employees of 2010 are undeniably different than the 20- and 30-something employees of 1970.

In fact, the evidence of this lies in the very fact that 10-15 years after the Xers first started shaking things up at the office, we are still discussing the differences and asking the same questions. They've grown up, settled down, had babies, progressed into management, achieved leadership roles and yet they are still ruffling feathers, and the Millennials below them are equally confounding … even to many Xers.

So we must recognize that this generational shift is a legitimate business and cultural trend stemming from real changes in technology, in the family dynamic, in the general affluence of our society, and in the social/political environment. The question, then, is this: How is business handling this very real trend?

David Zach, a futurist and business speaker, looks at fads, trends and principles as lenses through which one can view the world. They can overlap, but ultimately each has a distinct impact on business. David and I have connected on the speaker circuit, and his Fads, Trends, Principles Theory speaks to the challenges of generations in the workforce and the wait-it-out or work-it-out conundrum that many leaders still seem unsure how to answer.

FADS, TRENDS, PRINCIPLES THEORY

ACCORDING TO ZACH, fads often pretend to be trends. "Fads are all about being in a moment in time, particularly to enjoy that moment," he says. "We should play with fads because they can be fun and help us enjoy life. We can use fads to catch the attention of our customers and employees, but we need to keep them in perspective."

So fads are about popularity and attention. That's easy. It's the clothing and music that represent a moment in time. While members of one generation or another may either be drawn to or put off by a specific fad, they are also apt to flit from fad to fad with little attention or concern. Trends, on the other hand, are about movement and change over time, and as such are more enduring and important. They are changes such as advancements in technology, broader social attitudes, and demographic shifts. Trends reveal themselves over time and are not the momentary flash of so-called "popular" behavior or "must-have" accessory. Trends are where the generation-driven norms reside.

As Zach describes it, fads are the waves that rock the boat. Principles are the ever-consistent navigational stars. And trends are the currents that move the boat along its journey to a particular destination. "Trends take more effort to notice and can shape the overall direction of a society," Zach explains. "We work with trends because they are longer lasting and more influential and because that is where our work will do the most good."

Trends tend to have a beginning and end. For example, the trend toward the integration of technology into our lives began around 1969 with the invention of the microchip and has pretty well achieved saturation. There's no longer a trend to adopt technology because it is everywhere. Technology innovation continues, but the trend of technology impacting lives has run its course and everything is different as a result.

Generational difference in the workplace is likewise a trend, originating in the arrival of the Xers in corporate America in the mid-80s. It is a current that is rippling through the working world and making people question habits of recruiting, management and motivation that had become standard operating procedure.

But let's build upon Zach's metaphor a moment – if you were sailing toward a specific destination and the currents were moving you off course, what would you do? If the trends are pulling you in a different direction than you intended, how can you get back on course?

If you simply let the currents move you, you'll likely end up at the wrong destination. Going against the current will expend great amounts of energy and, in all likelihood, will remain futile. But if you skillfully navigate by knowing your enduring principles, they can guide you to work with the currents to reach your desired destination. You may not get there as directly as you supposed, but as long as you keep your principles in mind and your eyes open, you might just enjoy the journey while still getting to where you want to go. By knowing the difference between fads, trends, and principles, and how you should respond to each, you will better navigate the waves and currents and find your way to success.

That is the fundamental premise behind generational studies and generationally aware management strategies. The boat *is* moving. If you ignore why it is moving, you may miss your port of call. If you work with the changing current you can still reach your goal. The destination itself, like your company or individual principles, doesn't have to change. Only the approach is modified.

And there is our good news for struggling traditionalists: Principles don't bow down to trends. Though there is a trend right now regarding prevailing generational attitudes about how things such as loyalty, work ethic and time are expressed, these fundamental ideals are as reliable as the tides and as fixed as the North Star. Attitudes about them may ebb and flow over time, but those principles themselves do not change. So, if you know what you believe in, you are better able to defend and promote them within a framework that is understood and appreciated by other generations. Loyalty, for example, is a principle that will not go away, however it may be expressed in different ways by different generations.

It is easy to get where you are headed if you know who and where you are. That is, the fundamental truths of your organization are still solid and enduring, despite the changes occurring in the workforce. According to Zach, "Just as fads anchor you to a moment in time, principles can free you from time. ... They are not simply about this time, they are about all time."

FAD-TREND-PRINCIPLE THEORY APPLIED TO THE GENERATIONS

Fad: Pets welcome at workplace
Trend: Increased emphasis on self-expression and blurring of work/life boundaries
Principle: Consistent delivery of solid product and strong customer service.

In this situation, the fad is the outward expression of the trend, and it can be allowed as long as the principle is upheld. When/if having pets in the office interferes with delivering a solid product with strong customer service, that benefit will end … and a new way to meet the needs of the trend must be determined. Perhaps telecommuting options increase or new social outlets are created within the workplace. Guided by the trend, the fad itself is fluid. The principle never wavers.

BACK TO OUR TRAFFIC COP …

WHEN WE LAST looked in on David Houchins, he was stuck between a text and a scowl. How did he approach the generational crossroads? Head on.

"I realized that the Millennials at the table were not intentionally being rude; they were just being themselves. At the same time, I understood that the Xer and Boomer team members were essentially drawing a hard conclusion about their coworkers' commitment to the team. So I just laid it on the table," Houchins said.

"I told the Millennials, 'I know you are still listening while you text, and I know that you will take this information, incorporate it into your sales strategies and go gangbusters with it. So your actions right now do not bother me. However, not everyone sees it that way and you need to know that. While you multitask well, and in fact it seems you probably need to multitask to process information, the rest of the team sees multitasking as a distraction and assumes a lack of commitment on your part. And that may come back to haunt you."

In having this conversation with his team, Houchins was able to convey dual messages:

To the Boomers (and some Xers): I understand and appreciate that you may be irritated on my behalf. However, this behavior does not bother me in that respect.

To the Millennials: I understand and appreciate that you are able to listen and text simultaneously and are not intentionally being rude. However, by most accounts your behavior is perceived as rude and you run that risk of guilt by association if you choose to continue it.

To his delight, the air cleared and both sides were able to move ahead as a team. This is one small example of how generational perspective can color the same situation as viewed by different individuals. As I travel the country speaking to businesses about generational differences, I share stories like Houchins' and invariably someone comes up after the presentation to say, "You could have been talking to about me up there." Interestingly, that applies to ALL segments of the workforce – Matures, Boomers, Xers, and Millennials.

ARE THE GENERATIONS REALLY ALL THAT DIFFERENT?

IN A WORD, yes. They have different historical experiences that shape their expectations about life, technology, work, etc. We'll talk more about that in the next chapter. However, it is important to understand that the distinction is genuine and is consistently reported by businesses across the country, and even worldwide. Simply stated, Gen Xers and Millennials want a different work experience than the ones their parents had. And more than simply desiring this change, they expect and demand it. Most disturbing, if they cannot find the experience they desire, they will move on. Even in a tough economy it is not uncommon to see a dissatisfied employee, probably an Xer or Millennial, pick up and go. After all, they were told to "go find a good job that makes you happy" and many are trying to do just that, regardless of the wisdom of that decision.

In fact, in 2008, the Bureau of Labor reported that 65 percent of employees surveyed indicated they would leave their company within one year. This is up from 39 percent in the 1993 study.[1] In 15 short years, the number of people anticipating mobility in their careers nearly doubled. People are on the move, so we need to work quickly to engage them, hoping to gain more years of service and more return for our human resources investment. On average, 13 percent of a company's employees will leave each year, resulting in a 50 percent workforce turnover every four years.[2] With the cost of replacing an employee estimated at anywhere from two to 30 times annual salary, the burden to retain and engage employees remains squarely on the company.

So what is it that Xer and Millennial workers really want? It depends on the generation and their age within the generation, but most of the changes revolve around shifting definitions and expectations of time, loyalty, connection, responsibility and growth. These younger employees are indeed looking for a job that makes them happy, and they yearn to be loyal to that job or boss, yet they have no expectation of company loyalty and lifelong employment. They are ready to work hard to get the job done, but they don't necessarily want to work standard business hours. They want to see opportunities for fast advancement in pay and/or responsibility, but they don't want to be confined by a single-track career path.

Yes, they unequivocally want to have their cake and eat it too. The good news is that cake is meant to be eaten. There are ways to adjust your business or management style to accommodate Gen X and Millennial demands while remaining true to your fundamental business and principles.

IT'S ALL HOW YOU LOOK AT IT

A LOCAL PBS affiliate used to run a between-the-shows segment where an everyday household item was shown in tight focus and a group of children off camera guessed what it was. The camera slowly pulled back and the perspective changed. Ultimately, the children would realize that what they thought was a bowl of spaghetti was actually the head of a mop, and with cheery voices they would proclaim, "It's all how you look at it."

The same may be said of the generations at work. At first glance, a situation appears one way, but upon deeper inspection, it can be something else entirely. It's all how you look at it. And the best way to look at things is from the perspective of the other person – in this case, the different generations.

Let's look at some recent survey results and consider the different ways each can be viewed:

▶ *64 percent of college students surveyed expect to be promoted within 18 months of landing their first job.*[3]
First glance: They are impatient and not willing to pay their dues.
Closer look: They are motivated and seek advancement opportunities.

▶ *More than 40 percent of working fathers think employers do not provide enough family leave benefits.*[4]
First glance: They are not committed to work.
Closer look: Fathers also seek work/life balance.

▶ *62 percent of 18-26 year olds prefer to work for a company that provides opportunities to apply their skills to benefit nonprofits.*[5]
First glance: They want to be paid for personal interests.
Closer look: They want to make a difference while building business skills.

These are but a few examples of how attitudes and actions of a generation can lead to inaccurate assumptions. In fact, my conversations with executives, managers, and workers around the globe have taught me that the faulty assumptions are universal. Everyone, that is, every generation, seems to be looking around and saying, "Nobody gets me," or "I don't understand them." It is not a one-way confusion. Xers don't get Boomers or Millennials. Boomers don't understand Millennials or Xers. And Millennials don't relate to Boomers or Xers. The solution must be 360-degrees of understanding, right?

Yes and no.

Ideally everyone would take the time to better understand everyone else; Millennials would accept and adapt to the needs of their Boomer bosses, while Boomers would accommodate the demands of their younger employees. However, as I tried to impress upon Manager A, the numbers just don't support the need for bottom-up adaptation. Yes, the Boomers represent the largest generation and hold the majority of power in today's business world. However, they are already beginning to retire and the generations behind them simply do not have the numbers to fill the void. In 2008 the Bureau of Labor statistics estimated that by 2010 there would be 161 million jobs and approximately 154 million workers.[6] Outside of financially driven layoffs, the employment power lies in the hands of the younger generations.

WHY IS THIS SO IMPORTANT?

THE BUYER'S MARKET on employment is a new phenomenon. Traditionally, the boss positioned the hoops and the employees dutifully jumped through them. If they didn't like it or couldn't fit, tough luck, there were plenty of willing candidates lined up behind them. This is the world that Boomers entered as graduates and have experienced all their working lives. With 80 million peers, the competition was always in sight and the idea of making demands of the company – especially early in one's career – was unheard of until recently.

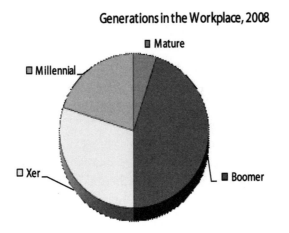

Generations in the Workplace, 2008

Today, there is a greater percentage of college-educated and technically trained candidates flooding the job market; however, the overall numbers are much smaller. Generation X has a mere 44 million members. And while the Millennials, at 75 million strong, are close in number to the Boomers, fewer than 50 percent of this generation are currently of employment age.[7] The combined total of both Xers and Millennials currently of working age is roughly equal to the entire Boomer population.

This means that as Boomers retire, the younger generations are going to need to work smarter in order to maintain the momentum of the past 30 years. In fact, "smarter, not harder" is practically the rallying cry of the Xer generation. So it continues to make sense that business evolves to meet the styles and expectation of the younger generations.

BUT ISN'T IT REALLY DEPENDENT ON THE ECONOMY?

SINCE LATE 2008, this question has been top of mind for business leaders. In an economic slowdown, don't the tables turn and shift the power back to the business? If these young, hard-to-please workers aren't able to walk out one door and see 10 others open before them, don't they just have to get with the program and deal with the traditional values of the Boomers who have set the pace for today's business?

Perhaps on the front end. It is true that when budgets are tightened and perks must be reigned in, some of the desires and demands of the newly employed must be put on the back burner. *I would argue that an employee who stays in the job because of lack of alternatives is still not an engaged, productive employee who will contribute to the long-term success of your business.* He may meet expectations to ensure employment, but at the first opportunity, he will jump ship.

The collective histories that make up our generational stereotypes, or norms, are very real. And they are within each employee whether or not the time is right to act on them. As a result, I would caution every business to continue to look at the needs of each generation and determine how you can meet them at some level. Even the U.S. government has had to deal with this same issue.

As was widely publicized at the time of his inauguration, President Obama was hesitant to surrender his Blackberry, per traditional security procedures that require the president to give up direct personal communications. As a young Boomer, President Obama was well accustomed to technology in daily life and he relied heavily on the device to maintain contact with his family, friends, and peers. In a nod to generational differences, the White House created a new protocol for changing times. While the president still had to surrender his personal e-mail and Blackberry, he was issued a new mobile device with the latest security features and restricted use. In effect, they met him where he was. To be sure, President Obama was not about to abandon his post over the ability to text message, but the efforts made to dovetail the desires of a tech-savvy president with the security needs of the country echo the recommendation to identify opportunities to meet the expectations of the individual while protecting the needs of the business.

And what, exactly, are these expectations? A 2007 study commissioned by Yahoo! HotJobs and Robert Half International and widely reported upon in business trend circles reveals precisely what the younger generations expect from the workplace.[8]

JOB CHOICE CONSIDERATIONS

Survey participants were asked to rate the following areas in terms of how important they are when considering a job or job offer:

Ranked 1-10, with 10 being the highest

Salary	9.05
Benefits (health insurance, 401(k), etc.)	8.86
Opportunities for career growth/advancement	8.74
The company's location	8.44
Company leadership	7.95
The company's reputation/brand recognition	7.56
Job title	7.19
In-house training programs	6.95
Tuition reimbursement programs	6.44
The diversity of the company's staff	6.07
The company's charitable/philanthropic efforts	6.06

DESIRED BENEFITS AND PERKS:

Millennial respondents ranked benefits as they pertain to their overall job satisfaction:

Healthcare coverage	9.02
Vacation (paid time off)	8.82
Dental care coverage	8.80
401 (k) program	8.58
Bonuses	8.25
Flexible working hours/telecommuting	8.06
Profit-sharing plans	7.52
Subsidized training/education	7.51
Mentoring programs	6.41
Housing or relocation assistance	6.38
Free/subsidized snacks or lunch	6.02
Subsidized transportation	5.73
On-site perks (dry cleaning, fitness center, etc.)	5.59
Subsidized gym membership	5.59
Matching-gifts program	5.33
Sabbaticals	5.26
On-site childcare	4.92
Adoption assistance	4.05

SUCCESS & LOYALTY:

"How much time do you think professionals entering the workforce should have to spend 'paying their dues' in entry-level positions?"

Less than one year	16%
One to two years	51%
Two to three years	19%
More than three years	5%
Not sure	9%

"How long do you expect to stay at your current position?"

Less than one year	16%
One to two years	24%
Three to five years	19%
Six years or more	22%
Not sure	19%

Gen Y respondents ranked the following aspects of their work environment on a one-to-10 scale, with 10 being the most important and one the least important.

A manager I can respect and learn from	8.74
Working with people I enjoy	8.69
Having work/life balance	8.63
Having a short commute	7.55
Working for a socially responsible company	7.42
Having a nice office space	7.14
Working with state-of-the-art technology	6.89

Looking through these stats it's clear the younger employees have high expectations. They want good salaries, solid benefits and a degree of flexibility. They want to work in a strong community environment and they don't expect to stay still very long. What these stats don't tell you is that they expect to move because they don't hold much faith that companies can or are willing to meet their needs. Therefore, if the expectations are met, they will stay still or will at least look within the company. Generational restlessness does not have to mean losing your talent investment to another company. If you've created a foundation of trust by meeting some of their basic expectations, perhaps in new and unusual ways, they will be more likely to seek change from within.

Next up, we'll talk a little about why these expectations exist – how it is that each generation in the workplace has emerged with such distinct characteristics – and then we will jump right into strategies for engaging your workforce and keeping your talent despite these differences.

TO THINK ON...

- **ARE THERE BEHAVIORS** you notice around your workplace that you assume are characteristic of a certain generation's attitude about their job? Could these behaviors be interpreted differently? Are there credible reasons for this behavior? Have you made a snap judgment?

- **DO YOU FEEL THAT** employees should act the way you did when you were that age? In that position? Had that responsibility? Do you feel that way because that is the way you or someone else did that job? Are you allowing a different procedure cloud the fact that progress is being made?

- **WHILE GENERATIONAL** differences are certainly cause for reflection on how you manage and motivate people, they are not an excuse for poor performance or unacceptable behavior. Have you set a limit for when you must intervene to help a person complete the job or find someone else for the position?

- **IF YOU'RE A PARENT** do you see some of these ideals manifesting themselves in your home? If so, is there any reason to believe that your children won't behave similarly in someone else's workplace? What about someone else's child?

CHAPTER TWO

HOW DID THIS HAPPEN

Communication, Work Habits and Expectations Continue to Shift

WITH AT LEAST THREE, and sometimes four, generations working side by side, it is important to understand both how they are similar and how they are different. The premise behind generational research and generation-driven management strategies is that shared histories shape the collective identity of each generation. In other words, the political, economic, and cultural happenings they experienced together combine to form a generational DNA of sorts.

This colors their perspectives and defines their values. It's what makes a Mature trust institutions and an Xer shy away from authority. What's more, it is an honest difference from generation to generation, rather than a personality defect among one or the other. So let's take a few moments to look at exactly what makes each generation tick.

Before we go too far into generational profiling, though, it bears mentioning that not every individual within a generation fits every generational stereotype. There will always be the 35-year-old Xer who has a decidedly traditional Boomer mindset about work, just as there are Boomers who are tech-savvy, altruistic, free thinkers – characteristics we usually associate with Millennials.

Of course personal history also shapes our outlook and forms our individual personalities and preferences. Additionally, there are several subsets that tend not to reflect their generational norms because their life circumstances carry more influence than their age brackets – farmers, immigrants, former military, the extremely wealthy or impoverished, and firstborn children often fall under that category. However, the majority of individuals display at least a portion of the attitudes, characteristics, and ideals that mirror their same-age peers. This means they have similar work habits and workplace expectations. These generational profiles simply provide a framework for understanding.

It is also worth noting that it is usually the events of a generation's formative (pre-working) years that shape these norms. These are the events that the generations following cannot experience. Shared phenomena, such as the war in Iraq, may be common to everyone, yet their generational impact is still greatest on those members of society who are in their late teens/early twenties at the time. For example, while Boomers experienced the PC boom, Xers are defined by it – they were the ones in college and entering the workforce as computers were changing the world. Similarly, Matures largely observed Vietnam, while draft-eligible Boomers had their lives fundamentally changed by it.

So let's take a quick look at each generation and how they got where they are today.

MEET THE MATURES (BORN 1945 AND PRIOR)

When you think of this generation think:
Duty, Sacrifice

Formative events:
The Great Depression, Pearl Harbor, WW II, Hiroshima

Famous Matures:
George H.W. Bush, Jimmy Carter, John Glenn, Billy Graham, Charlton Heston

MATURES ARE ACTUALLY a combination of two generations, the Veterans (1901 – 1924) and the Silent Generation (1925 – 1945), whose characteristics in the workplace are very similar. They either fought in World War II or were children during the war. The eldest members of the Matures remember the Great Depression and their memories of those times have made an indelible mark on them. Many of their behaviors today can be traced back to their experiences during the Depression.

Of the four generations, the Matures are the smallest and the wealthiest. They either first entered the workforce during WWII or came home from the war and got a job with companies that took care of their employees. Both the company and the employee believed that loyalty to one another created even more loyalty. Most of the Matures worked for only one company in their lifetime and stayed with that employer until retiring, when the company rewarded them with a gold watch and a solid pension. The post-war workplace they inhabited was primarily male dominated. The mothers stayed at home, kept up the house and raised the children.

MATURES IN THE WORKPLACE

THOUGH MOST MATURES have entered retirement, their workplace habits and values have certainly shaped the company environment as witnessed by Boomers and Xers over their lifetimes. Today, some Matures are finding themselves back in the workforce – often part-time or on a consultant basis – as a result of either financial demands or simply relief from the boredom of a long retirement. Whether Matures are active in your workplace or they have simply left their mark on it, their traditional take on the workplace is still felt at many organizations. As a group, Matures

- Are loyal to their employer and expect the same in return.
- Typically possess superb interpersonal skills and, therefore, are often the best customer service providers in an organization.
- Enjoy flex-time arrangements today so they can work on their own schedules.

- Believe promotions, raises, and recognition should come from job tenure.
- Measure a work ethic on timeliness, productivity, and not drawing attention to oneself.

MEET THE BOOMERS (BORN 1946–1964)

When you think of this generation think:
Individuality, the first Me Generation, conspicuous consumption

Formative events:
The Civil Rights movement; assassinations of John F. Kennedy, Robert *Kennedy and Martin Luther King Jr.; Vietnam War; Woodstock; The Cold War; Roe vs. Wade*

Famous Boomers:
Muhammad Ali, The Beatles, Bill Clinton, Katie Couric, Bill Gates, Indra Nooyi, Arnold Schwarzenegger, Oprah Winfrey

TODAY, THE BOOMERS are in control. They run our local, state, and national governments; they are the bosses, supervisors, managers, and CEOs of most companies; and they dominate the workforce because of their enormous numbers. They are prized employees because of their dedication to a solid, strong work ethic that is uniquely defined by them as "working long and hard and being seen doing it." The word "workaholic" was coined to describe the Boomers. They advocate face time, believing that one must be seen working hard or else that hard work doesn't really count.

Whereas Matures laid the groundwork for the United States to become an influential member of the world community, Boomers came behind and set the wheels in motion. Through their enormous numbers, their intense work ethic, and their competitive nature, the Boomers got productive and brought the United States to the forefront of the world economic engine. Boomers also believe in the sanctity and the importance of the individual. Developing oneself into a more "whole" person is very important. You will see this come to bear in the attitudes of their children (hint: the Millennials and many Xers). Part of becoming a better person is learning to operate as a fluid member of a team, and the Boomers are champions of teamwork.

Boomers today are still working as hard as they've ever worked but some are asking themselves if their intense work ethic has paid off the way they had hoped. One big reason for this shift is that Boomers entered the workplace when company loyalty was still standard. They've seen that change dramatically as tough economic conditions have required layoffs and downsizings. Their noteworthy work ethic may have ultimately gone unrewarded. They are left wondering if they've missed critical parts of their personal lives while giving the company 110 percent.

The Boomers are evolving and in the second halves of their lives will live with a different focus. Many Boomers are eager to begin their "encore" careers, where they'll leave behind their vocation – which was necessary to pay the bills and clothe the kids – and begin their avocation where the work, the pace, and the location will be of their choosing. They are beginning to follow their own advice and are going out to find jobs that make them happy.

BOOMERS IN THE WORKPLACE

BOOMERS STILL COMPOSE the majority of leadership roles in the nation's workforce, though retirement is fast approaching, if not already arrived. They built upon the traditional views of their Mature predecessors and turned work into a badge of honor. During their reign the American economy has largely flourished, though not without costs. As employees and leaders, Boomers:

- Believe in, champion, and evaluate themselves and others based on their proven work ethic.
- Measure work ethic in actual time on the job, i.e., hours. Actual productivity in those hours may be less important.
- Believe teamwork is critical to success and are excellent consensus builders.
- Place a high value on face time and relationship building.
- Expect loyalty from their coworkers and staff.

- Believe that good team members are those who are willing to dedicate whatever time is needed to get the job done and to support the team.

MEET THE XERS (BORN 1965-1979)

When you think of this generation think:
Skeptical, reluctant, self-sufficient, most loyal consumers, most loyal employees

Formative events:
Watergate, fall of the Berlin Wall, Challenger explosion, the Gulf War, the PC Boom, the Reagan Presidency, Clinton/Lewinsky Scandal

Famous Xers:
Andre Agassi, David Beckham, Sara Blakely, Kurt Cobain, Michael Dell, Jon Favreau, Bobby Jindal, Jenny McCarthy, Chris Rock

THIS GENERATION CAME onto the scene and was given an extremely vague name: Generation X. They were defined as slackers and characterized as unmotivated, lethargic, sarcastic, and irreverent. They were the first generation that parents could take pills not to have. And as youths they were told they'd be the first generation in the nation's history that would not be as successful as their parents. Every institution in the United States that has said, "You can trust us" – government, the church, military, marriage, major corporations – has fallen flat on its face at some point during Xer youth. Whereas to the Boomers and Matures these institutions still mean a great deal despite some setbacks, to Xers they have never been deserving of anything but skepticism.

Though they could easily be considered pessimistic about their world and their future, upon digging deeper you'll find that the Xer attitude has a "carpe diem" feel to it. "There is nothing we can count on in the future," they say, "so we'll focus short term and make sure each day has significance." It is not an attitude of irresponsibility. It is actually the contrary: Xers have willingly shouldered the responsibility for their own day-to-day well-being. "We've seen that the company won't provide it, nor will the government," they think, "So it is up to me." This attitude permeates the workplace where Xers are steadily rejecting the Boomer work ethic attitude. Ironically, they're gaining Boomer converts along the way.

Many of the eldest Xers are now firmly entrenched in management positions and the youngest have been in the workplace for several years now. Their attitudes and viewpoints are no longer new. Xers will continue to inherit management positions vacated by retiring Boomers (if their go-getter Millennial peers don't leapfrog over them), and they'll run things a bit differently. Don't fear; they'll be effective, profitable, and responsible ... but different.

XERS IN THE WORKPLACE

THE XER BRINGS a strong set of ideals to the workplace, defying convention and reinventing the status quo. Their entrepreneurial spirit was bolstered by the surge of the dot-com era where start-up companies embraced quirky work environments and informal organizational charts. As they age, Xers are beginning to seek stability but are unwilling to surrender individual freedoms to achieve it. As both managers and employees, they:

- Eschew the hard-core, super-motivated, do or die Boomer work ethic.
- Want open communication regardless of position, title, or tenure.
- Respect productivity over tenure.
- Value control of their time.
- Look for a person, not a company, to whom they can invest loyalty.

MEET THE MILLENNIALS (BORN 1980-2000)

When you think of this generation think:
Idealistic, group-oriented, well cared for, confident, pressured, conventional, stressed, high-achieving.

Formative events:
Oklahoma City bombing, 9/11 terrorist attack, the Internet boom, mobile technology, No Child Left Behind, Amber Alerts, "Baby on Board"

Famous Millennials:
Christina Aguilera, Natalie Portman, Justin Timberlake, Serena and Venus Williams, Princes William and Harry of Windsor, Elijah Wood

BORN IN A TIME when cell phones, laptops, remote controls, satellite feeds and videoconferencing are the norm, Millennials are living in a world of ubiquitous technology. And the studies show they'll still see more change in their lifetime than any other generation. Along with ever-present technology, Millennials have mostly known national affluence in their lives, regardless of personal situations. The recent economic downturns are the first declines in the nation's economic pace they've ever experienced. Depending on the length and severity of the recession, it may or may not have a lasting impact on Millennial actions and attitudes.

Largely children of the Boomers and the oldest Xers, the Millennials have been widely protected by their parents. As children, they were subject to a new and unwieldy manner of threat, different than any other generation – rogue individuals with nuclear weapons, unchecked violence from their peers, and terrorism in their own nation (and, in one case, by their own countrymen). Their parents' response was to insulate and protect their children, to carefully guide them through life, and to constantly build their self-esteem.

This is the generation where participation awards emerged for every activity, telling children, "It doesn't matter if you win or lose; you showed up so here is a trophy." This is craziness to the older generations, while completely normal to and expected by the Millennials. Their lives thus far are epitomized by the yellow "Baby on Board" signs displayed on nearly every minivan and station wagon throughout the '80s and '90s. Their parents warned the world to be mindful of precious cargo, and the message was well-received. Millennials grew up believing they were all special.

Today, the Millennials are entering the workforce in droves. A population whose size will rival the Boomers, the Millennials come into the workplace looking for the opportunity to learn and move about. They want to be close to their peers and seek leadership from their bosses and supervisors. They are an army waiting to be guided, but they play by different rules.

MILLENNIALS IN THE WORKPLACE

AS MILLENNIALS JOIN the working world, they leave behind environments created to cater to their needs, be it the family home or the college dorm. As a result, many are coming to the office with high expectations for customization, yet they also have a strong desire to leave their mark. This generation places a high value on achievement, creating a great opportunity for companies who learn to tap into this key generational dynamic. As a collective workforce, Millennials:

- Search for the individual who will help them achieve their personal goals.
- Want open, constant communication and positive reinforcement from their boss.
- Tend to work best with individuals from the Mature generation.
- Desire a job that provides great personal fulfillment.
- Are looking for ways to shed the stress in their lives.

So what does this mean for managers and businesses?

Evidence and anecdotes alike demonstrate a clear difference in how each generation performs in the workplace. The discord caused by these differences can be painful, as Manager A illustrated so well. When we look at the how and why of these disparities, it becomes easier to realize that each generation has come to define basic workplace terms and values in different ways. Loyalty, time, success, commitment — all have distinct meanings for each generation. By adapting management techniques to the underlying trends of the generations, we can begin to create a working environment that effectively appeals to each generation and each employee.

I created the following generational cheat sheet as a quick summary of high-level tactics that will help managers and organizations engage employees of each generation. Further ahead we will discuss real-world applications for many of these approaches.

TO ENGAGE MATURES

Managers Should...
- Take care not to "overdo" recognition, especially for simply doing what is expected.
- Be open to alternative schedules. Matures are now typically working because they want to, not because they have to. Retaining them may require flexibility.
- Understand and recognize the importance of teamwork. Matures believe the group is more powerful and more important than the individual.

Communications Should ...

• Be spoken and written. This is particularly important for messages that impact the company or their work.

• Use traditional formats. Text-messaging terms are considered rude and indecipherable.

• Come from tenured authority figures in the company.

• Clearly communicate what is needed from them and their teammates.

The Corporate Culture Should ...

• Allow Matures to feel confident and able regarding technology. Don't expect mastery without proper training.

• Operate under clear rules and expectations. Communicate changes properly to all.

• Provide opportunities to stay in touch with changing expectations, particularly technological skills.

• Value their institutional wisdom. Call upon Matures for guidance when appropriate; they are superb teachers.

Training Programs Should ...

• Be immediately and clearly relevant.

• Use their time wisely.

• Invite discussion throughout the training, including how the training will help and its implications on their work.

• Provide insights regarding their workplace peers and existing/potential clients.

• Be delivered by someone with "earned" authority, not someone who could be their grandchild (unless it is technology skills training).

Rewards and Recognition Should ...

• Celebrate the efforts of the whole team, not any single individual.

• Be genuine and sincere. Nothing beats a handshake and a personal "thank you" from the boss.

• Recognize true achievements, not simply rewards for doing the job.

TO ENGAGE BOOMERS

Managers Should ...
• Adopt a "get it done" and "whatever it takes" attitude.
• Be visible and active in the workplace. Boomers value face time and do not want to be managed from afar.
• Demonstrate how you have earned your leadership role.
• Have firsthand knowledge of subordinate's work, preferably having done the same job at some point.

Communications Should ...
• Highlight and celebrate team goals/accomplishments.
• Focus on team goals, preferably posted in public places where everyone can be reminded of them.
• Avoid text-messaging abbreviations.
• Demonstrate understanding of stated team goals and be focused on helping the team towards those goals.
• Be delivered in person where possible. E-mail is secondary.

The Corporate Culture Should ...
• Offer the tools Boomers need to do the job better, faster, and more thoroughly.
• Promote visibility of bosses and workplace peers. Face time matters.
• Acknowledge both individuals and teams who have achieved their goals.
• Promote collaborative meetings where everyone can provide input as desired.
• Allow Boomers time to anticipate and prepare for change.

Training Programs Should ...
• Keep Boomers up-to-date and competitive in a quickly changing workplace.
• Allow all levels of technology skills to learn without feeling inferior or intimidated.
• Pre-evaluate skills, don't assume.
• Be participatory and interactive, allowing for deliberation and discussion versus one-way instruction. Ask them more questions than they ask you.
• Create realistic examples to use in the learning process.

Rewards and Recognition Should …
- Celebrate the individual as well as the team.
- Be public and/or able to be displayed. Boomers value trophies, plaques, lapel pins, etc.
- Encourage celebrations within the team as well as companywide acknowledgements.

TO ENGAGE XERS

Managers Should …
- Honor commitments at all cost. Gen Xers place a high value on reliability.
- Recognize that work does not equal life. Celebrate Xers' hobbies or passions in addition to their work skills.
- Allow for flexibility and negotiate individual schedules.
- Regularly review individual and team goals, and the individual's role on the team.
- Revisit deadlines as needed.

Communications Should …
- Get straight to the point. Gen Xers loathe fluff.
- Be consistent and supported with actions as well as words. The company must walk their talk every day.
- Be infrequent. Official corporate communications should be saved for critical messages.
- Be individualized and delivered personally.
- E-mail is usually the preferred method of communication followed by face-to-face conversation.

The Corporate Culture Should …
- Trust their time-management skills. Check in regularly but not frequently.
- Allow them to get their work done without interference or unnecessary interruptions. Leave them alone when they're focused on their tasks.
- Seek their input frequently on what you can do to make things better, easier, faster.
- Respond to their requests with actions and results.

Training Programs Should ...

• Address the employee's career goals. Ask "What skills do you need to get where you want to go?"
• Be flexible. Gen Xers want information and choices.
• Demonstrate commitment to "work smarter, not harder."
• Include leaders and peers, demonstrating management's commitment to the training as a valuable use of time.
• Promote new ideas on how to get things done.

Rewards and Recognition Should ...

• Offer variety. Allow Gen Xers to choose from a list of reward options with roughly equal values.
• Express gratitude for the individual's contribution in private. Xers don't want a fuss for doing their jobs.
• Honor commitments to goals that are solid and achievable. Don't keep upping the ante or you lose trust.

TO ENGAGE MILLENIALS

Managers Should ...

• Have a sincere interest in the individual. Spend time with them and get to know their goals and personalities.
• Commit to helping them develop new, valuable, and relevant skills.
• Recognize that work does not equal life. Have fun.
• Offer scheduling flexibility with negotiations (Like Gen X).
• Articulate how working for you will help them achieve their personal goals while also benefitting the company.

Communications Should ...

• Outline the steps needed to achieve a goal.
• Establish checkpoints along the way to document progress toward goals and provide frequent feedback.
• Celebrate individual contributions to team goals.
• Be positive. When giving criticism be prepared with a 3:1 positive-to-negative ratio – three compliments for every one reprimand.

The Corporate Culture Should ...
- Ask "What have you learned today? Anything you think I need to know?"
- Avoid strict hierarchy/chains of command.
- Seek input from everyone, not just those with big titles.
- Encourage optional social activities that are open to all employees and are held outside the office after hours. Adopt and develop an employee social calendar.
- Give credit to individuals for their ideas and involvement.

Training Programs Should ...
- Involve the whole group, where practical.
- Clearly identify how they'll benefit from learning this information both at this job and beyond.
- Be interactive and fun.
- Allow everyone to take a role in some part of the teaching process.

Rewards and Recognition Should ...
- Offer options, similar to Gen X needs. Millennials cherish their individuality.
- Be celebrated publicly, in front of the team and/or visible to the customer where appropriate (lapel pin, etc).
- Offer special "top performer" learning opportunities to reward initiative and help propel employees toward their future goals.
- Happen during the work day. Validate the reward by celebrating on company time.

Remember, today's workforce is top heavy with Boomers who have followed in the footsteps of the Matures. Tomorrow's workforce will be lean, populated by Millennials and Xers who have a dramatically different outlook on the way work and life should interact. *To retain the legacies built by their Mature and Boomer leaders, companies must begin to shift the workplace culture in favor of Xer and Millennial ideals. And they must begin now.*

Indeed, over the next five, 10 and 15 years, the influence of Xers and Millennials cannot be overstated. Creating secure, engaged workforces now – and transferring knowledge from Boomers before they retire – will make the difference in whether companies will be able to last from generation to generation.

Luckily there are companies and managers out there who are ahead of the curve in dealing with generational differences, and we can look to them for guidance. In general, entrepreneurial business and industries that are rapidly expanding or are considered hot careers are the first to adapt to changing trends. For entrepreneurs, it is often because they are still nimble and able to adopt new policies and procedures on the fly, taking into consideration the precise needs of a defined workforce. The entrepreneurial spirit, too, is aligned with the idea of change and finding a new, better way to do things. For larger or more traditional industries, leaders are often pushed into finding new solutions because of demands from a competitive employee base. *To attract and retain top talent, you need to be the company and the manager that your employees want to support.*

Let's get started.

TO THINK ON...

• **WHICH GENERATION BEST** defines you? No one has the all the characteristics of their generation, but you'll typically find that your birth generation mostly defines you. How does it make you feel to know that there are millions of others with so many similarities?

• **IF YOU DO NOT** fit your generational profile, which one do you fit in? What explanations do you have for it?

• **BASED ON THE INFORMATION** provided, which generation would you want to be in if you could choose? Which generation would you want to manage? To be managed by?

• **CONSIDER YOUR WORKPLACE** peers/teammates – do they fall into their generational descriptions based on what you know about their age? If someone doesn't fit, what generation do they seem most like?

• **CONSIDER SOMEONE VERY** important to your success at your workplace and mentally place him or her in a particular generation. It would work best for the exercise if this is a person you're having workplace relationships or communications challenges with. Keep them in mind as you continue reading the book and see if you can't get some good ideas for working better with them.

• LASTLY, BEAR IN MIND that a person's generation is but one of many ways to understand someone's motivations and behaviors. There are many other things that make a person tick. What other things may influence someone's workplace behavior besides their generation?

CHAPTER THREE

GENERATION X COMES OF AGE

Becoming Parents, Gaining Responsibility – Where's the Balance?

FOR THE PAST 20 YEARS Gen Xers have been finding their footing in the work-force. The first to buck the trend of long hours and lots of face time, they were the generation that wanted to work hard *and* play hard, not wait until retirement to have all the fun. Joining the business world at the height of the technology expansion, they flitted from job to job, following interesting work, talented bosses, fabulous perks. They had all the time in the world and just wanted to enjoy it before they died.

Slacker.

The Boomers handed Xers this title when they first entered the workplace in early 1990. This new generation got to work no earlier than necessary, left on time, and only begrudgingly showed up in the office on the weekends, if at all. To the Boomers, with their "go-go-go" work ethic, these kids were slacking off. In truth, the Xers were introducing a new set of values to the workplace, one of balance and control over their lives. Their answer to the Boomers' accusations of slack? "We get more done in our forty hours of work than you do in your 55 hours. In fact, what in the world are you doing during the day that takes you so long to do your job. If we have a slack attitude, you must have time-management issues." And thus the lines were drawn nearly 20 years ago and, in many places, they remain today.

Today, Xers are in their 30s and 40s, and while their collective attitude and personality remains, priorities have changed. Mortgages, families, even retirement are on the table, or at least visible on the horizon, and stability has replaced excitement as a top career trait. They want longevity and advancement – on their terms. They may have postponed adulthood, but here they are. As a result, Xers are beginning to ask, "Can this career or company meet my needs and the needs of my family for the next 5+ years?" This is a great opportunity to encourage loyalty by making it possible for individuals to excel at the office while maintaining the flexibility to be committed to family.

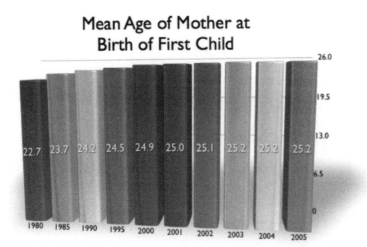

Mean Age of Mother at Birth of First Child

CDC Division of Vital Statistics[9]
This chart demonstrates the trend for women to have their first child at an older age than in the past. The mark has moved about three years over as many decades. What's the importance? In previous generations women were often done with their child bearing and rearing at a younger age than today. Xers and Millennials are starting this life stage later and it will last longer, as children are transitioning into self-sufficient adulthood at older ages, too. The point? If you're wishing the hassles of childcare issues at your workplace would just hurry up and go away, don't count on it. In fact, you should probably embrace it.

A NEW SENSE OF PURPOSE

WITH GEN XERS firmly in their child-raising years, definitions of work/life balance are shifting once again. Where Xers originally sought time to play and enjoy the world, they now seek balance in their family lives. Many Xers were raised by Boomer parents who were trained to put the job above all else and were rarely home – especially fathers. Today working mothers *and* fathers are making children the priority, demanding family leave, time off for volunteering at school, working odd hours to accommodate family schedules, and more. Yet, their dedication to the work is not fading – rather they are seeking different ways to accomplish it. *This is the generation that wants it all and believes that to be possible.*

As more and more Xers are supporting families, flexible schedules and job sharing become more important benefits. In a stroke of luck, these benefits are becoming increasingly important to the rest of the workforce as well. Boomers, whose children are primarily grown and on their own, are now facing elder-care responsibilities for aging parents and may want to spend more time with grandchildren. Matures, too, are looking for the freedom and flexibility to visit family and pursue personal interests. And the Millennials are strongly invested in exploring and living their lives outside of work. So flexibility as an Xer-driven benefit helps to meet the needs of a wide range of employee desires. Let's look at how some companies are making this happen.

TAKING THE WORRY OUT OF CHILDCARE

QUALITY CHILDCARE IS arguably the first and largest threat to productivity for working parents. There are so many factors to consider – cost, quality, reliability, convenience, availability – that it can seem daunting. Over the past decade, more and more companies are partnering with their employees in the search for affordable, high-quality childcare. They are telling employees, "Don't worry – we'll help you figure out what to do with Tyler all day. You stay committed to the job at hand."

This is not an entirely new phenomenon – manufacturing companies have a long history of providing some level of childcare to factory workers – but it is increasingly common among white-collar organizations, which traditionally employed males while their wives stayed home with the children. With dual-income and single-parent households on the rise, affordable childcare is now an issue for more employees, in more industries, than ever before.

Today, sharing the burden of childcare can take many incarnations, from providing childcare search support to opening on-site facilities for the children of employees; from assisting with childcare expenses to providing a sick room for children too ill to go to school but not so sick they need mom or dad to stay home.

Mitchell Gold + Bob Williams, a leading furniture manufacturer headquartered in Taylorsville, North Carolina, has taken easing the childcare burden to award-winning heights. In 1999, they invested more than $250,000 to establish Lulu's Child Enrichment Center (honoring the company's mascot, an English Bulldog named Lulu). The center is rated AAAA by the state of North Carolina and was named Provider of the Year for Alexander County. Prices for the daycare are based on a break-even point, and it is run as a rent-free, not-for-profit operation, making it an affordable care option for many of the company's 650 employees.[10]

In early 2009, a Mitchell Gold + Bob Williams representative was interviewed regarding the potential for downsizing perks (they also offer a free gym and chef-run cafeteria) as a result of soft markets. She asserted that these benefits have helped the company attract and retain high-quality workers and therefore remain worthwhile even as the home furnishings industry had been hit hard and people might be willing to accept lesser working conditions. "If you started stripping away some of those things, it would take away who we really are," the spokeswoman stated.[11]

Many other companies offer some level of on-site childcare. In fact, it is one of the criteria measured by Fortune for its Annual Best Companies list, with more than one-quarter of those recognized in 2008 offering on-site care. Such attention to the concerns of working parents is especially important when more than 50 percent of families have both parents working full time and the numbers of single parents is increasing. It is a benefit to the company to make manageable childcare a benefit to its workers.

Certainly not every company is able or willing to run its own on-site childcare facility. Still, there are other ways to make being a working parent easier. At Presbyterian Hospital in Charlotte, North Carolina, employees have access to Sniffles, a back-up childcare facility for situations when a child is too sick to go to school but not so sick that mom or dad needs to be home. Sniffles is staffed by nurses and available to all hospital employees for a per-day fee. This option is especially important in a hospital setting, where flextime or the use of PTO simply might not be options for some workers.

A more informal version of backup care works for a Boston-based start-up that matches care providers with individuals needing specific services. Employees' children have access to a dedicated playroom that can be used when a caregiver is unavailable or school is suddenly closed for inclement weather. The option allows parents to meet obligations to both work and family without interrupting the rest of the staff with children running amok.

For this company, whose entire business is built around helping others, the playroom is ideal. An employee reports that this low-cost solution works for everyone at the small office, which has a good mix of parent and nonparent employees. Yes, it uses up office space, but it also provides peace of mind, which ultimately improves productivity.

TAKEAWAYS

Help alleviate a top concern for working parents by assisting them with finding quality, affordable childcare, making it easier for them to return to work with confidence and focus on the task at hand. Consider the following approaches:

- Open an on-site daycare for children of employees
- Research local care providers and make that information available to parents
- Provide childcare expense reimbursements
- Offer drop-in care for emergency situations (ill child and/or primary care provider unavailable)
- Designate a child-friendly space in the office for occasional care needs

---

A ROADMAP TO THE "MOMMY TRACK"

IT IS NO SECRET that the decision to continue working or not after adding children to the family is a difficult one. Mothers, especially, are torn between being a SAHM (stay-at-home mom) or a WOHM (work-outside-the-home mom) and the impact on business is huge. When mothers leave the workforce, they take their training investment with them. If they wish to return to work once a child is older they risk losing traction as the business world surges ahead. And if they choose to continue working –for personal, professional or financial reasons, the logistics can be overwhelming. For this reason, companies can benefit from taking a more direct role in helping women make the transition.

Flexibility and support are critical to helping a new mother find her own way to balance her career and her family, should she desire. This is a professional-personal struggle that affects all genders and generations, but is heightened among the women of Gen X at the moment.

Roughly 25 years ago, Plante & Moran, the nation's 12th largest certified public accounting and business advisory firm and an 11-year honoree on Fortune's "Best Companies to Work For" list, recognized the need to support its staff members facing the dilemma of juggling career and family. By most accounts, they were way ahead of the curve. At the time, Plante & Moran created the Parental Tightrope Action Committee, a group charged with helping working mothers balance baby care with their careers. With women making up roughly half of their workforce, and the accounting profession overall at that time, it was imperative that the firm help women find their place when family entered the picture. The PTA Committee asked itself and its target audience:

- What policies are already in place?
- What do staff members need to know to enact these policies?
- What do parents need?
- What do existing parent staff members wish they had known in the beginning?

The result of their findings was the Plante & Moran Baby Book. Through the years, the book has been updated and the PTA committee has been re-established as the Personal Tightrope Action Committee, recognizing that everyone needs balance, not just working parents. The book remains true to its core principle, making navigation of work/life balance easier for all Plante & Moran staff members.

Plante & Moran
"We Care"

I know you are dying to know what is in the book. Everything. The tabbed binder, which is handed to expecting mothers and fathers (as well as others who may be facing a life transition and need additional insight on company policy and local resources) gives detailed information to help manage life-changing times:

- Leave of absence policies and requirements
- Benefits details and procedures
- Childcare resources
- Options for nontraditional work arrangements
- Dependent care tax issues and information
- Helpful hints and research from various parenting experts
- Useful forms and checklists – such as questions to ask daycares, nanny applications, etc.

Why would a firm go through all of this research and effort in an area not directly associated with work? According to Michelle Kolb, a regional HR specialist with Plante & Moran, the payoff is in the relief staff members express when they realize that their employer wants to make it work. "When I learn of an expecting parent in my region, the first thing I do is bring them 'the book,' as it is affectionately known at the firm," Kolb said. "They are just so excited to learn that there is something to help them through this crazy time and that the firm has already thought of almost everything and is willing to help. I see an immediate release of anxiety. *They aren't wondering if they can make it work anymore – now they see it is possible.* In fact, several of our female partners were once on a tailored work arrangement and they still made it to partner. It is part of our culture that women are not penalized for having children, and that takes a huge weight off the shoulders of new parents because they have real-world role models. "

The PTA Committee at Plante & Moran takes new parent assistance one step further with a mentoring program of sorts. The PTA Buddy is a veteran working parent who has agreed to help a new mother or father navigate the merging of parenthood and professionalism. Staff buddies are not required, but they are made available to those who would like an experienced shoulder to lean on. Individuals who volunteer as PTA buddies are provided with additional information and guidance on how to handle some of the questions that tend to come up. Human resources staff members also review the company policies and any recent updates, so firm-related information is communicated consistently.

As with the Baby Book, the buddy program has the overall effect of making new parents feel connected and supported. The book greatly appeals to the Xers' desire to have information at hand, digest it and make decisions in her own time. The buddy system also fits perfectly with the Millennial desire to be connected to peers and have a guiding hand. No matter which generation, the two programs demonstrate a comprehensive, and yet incredibly low cost, way of showing staff members how to navigate major life transitions while retaining their professional careers.

"We want to make sure that we retain promotional opportunities, especially for our female staff, when they face major life changes," Kolb said. "Through the 25 years the Personal Tightrope Committee has been in existence we continually look at the needs of the next generation, reflect on the experiences of the current staff, and make adjustments. The essence is ingrained in our corporate culture and the details continue to morph so that it continues to work for our staff. We are looking at broader applications – such as researching elder care resources – to make the book valuable to an even more staff members."

TAKE AWAYS

Major life stages, most noticeably the start of a family, have a definitive impact on an individual's professional life and the company as a whole. Show prospective parents you value their contributions to the workforce and are looking forward to their continued tenure with the company using proactive measures that demonstrate your support.

- Talk to current employees about what they wish they had known.
- Look at your company demographics to forecast likely upcoming transitions.
- Form a committee to research resources, including focused internal policies, for a variety of applicable situations.
- View transitions as an opportunity to create employee loyalty, not a burden to the company performance.
- Create a central resource for all company policies related to major life stages, consider including local external resources and references as well.
- Clearly state your intentions to ease the transition. Will you provide flexible scheduling, adjust responsibilities, renegotiate career tracks, offer parental perks? Let them know. In person.
- Publicize availability of support – if you don't make it visible and back it up, it's just talk.

A HODGEPODGE OF FAMILY-FRIENDLY BENEFITS

SOME OF THE DOT-COM era perks that were so wildly publicized and often created to meet younger Xers' demand for work/fun balance can morph into strong family balance perks today. That video console in the conference room? Perfect for keeping an elementary student occupied while he recovers from tonsillitis. The daily dry cleaning service? It minimizes the after-work errand cycle, allowing parents to spend more time with their children without taking away from work.

The underlying theme is to identify a way that your business can help its Xer parents have it all. Because, quite frankly, they expect it. As demanding as that sounds, you should embrace it while you can because they will return the favor in spades.

What if you really think outside the box and go waaaaay long term? The addition of children to the Xer world also brings things such as long-term financial planning into view. College education, retirement, life insurance – all things that were just floating in the periphery come into laser focus. Often this reality slap upside the head catches Xers unawares. At IBM, they are helping employees navigate this reality with a relatively new program dubbed MoneySmart.[12]

Now, I know what you are thinking – why would a company have to tell its employees how to manage their money? And is that even smart? Well, IBM isn't telling them; they are simply offering free phone access to financial advisers; the advice itself comes from the experts. And it *is* smart. Here's why – a stressed employee is generally not a great employee, and finances are one of the top causes of stress, especially among younger generations who were offered pre-approved credit card applications alongside their college course selections. Some expert advice is often appreciated.

Another great aspect of the MoneySmart program is that it is a benefit with universal appeal, albeit for a wide range of reasons. Millennials, though they may not be as stressed about the future, will be more likely to look into long-term savings vehicles such as 401(k) – they have no illusions of retirement supported by the company pension. Boomers may be seeking advice on their upcoming retirements or perhaps looking into options for long-term care insurance for older family members. Regardless of the reason, this is a creative benefit that, once again, offers long-term peace of mind for a range of employees.

Enterprise Rent-A-Car has also taken an outside-the-box approach to supporting families. The company has a National Diversity Team, which several years ago created a Family Focus Team to take a closer look at how Enterprise could better support its employees. Similar to Plante & Moran's Personal Tightrope Action Committee, the Enterprise team looks at a variety of ways that the company can help employees manage customary times of transition. The team discovered that, as a retail establishment, one of their recurring issues was relocation. Proven managers are moved to areas needing greater support or to new locations looking for a strong start. Enterprise had a solid relocation team in place to help employees with moving to a new area, including help with the actual logistics of moving. The Enterprise employee was always warmly welcomed at the new location and supported through the transition. What the Family Focus Team realized, however, was that spouses were often left to fend for themselves.

The resulting initiative – the Enterprise Spouse Relocation Team – reaches out to that employee's family to offer the kind of insight about a new location that is only available by living there. Where's a good dry cleaner? How are the schools? Who can refer a dentist or chiropractor or pediatrician? The spouse relocation team helps find the answers and serves as a local touchpoint for the uprooted spouse, easing the transition to a new home and making it easier for the employee to focus on the job, knowing that family is being helped as well. Each Enterprise group throughout the country has one or two individuals who have volunteered to serve in this capacity.

TAKEAWAYS

Supporting employees through life transitions can take many incarnations. Creative thinking can help identify cost-effective ways to help keep employees engaged when their life circumstances might have them distracted. Not only will this improve productivity, but it will also increase loyalty to the organization. These transitions are inevitable. Prepare yourself and your workplace for them and then show your staff that you mean it.

- Survey employees to determine anxiety points – financial planning, elder care, dependent care, housing, health/wellness, etc.
- Tap into existing resources – your employees – to identify anxiety-relief strategies.
- Create a "coworker certified" resource list for recommended service providers, including electricians, plumbers, handyman, lawn care, physicians, etc. and make it available through HR or the company intranet.
- Host occasional brown bag lunches on topics of interest – organic gardening, marathon training, etc.
- Look internally and externally for possible low-cost, high-return solutions. Can you …
- Partner with a local exercise facility?
- Offer smoking cessation classes during lunch breaks?
- Assign staff to research child/elder care resources?
- Partner with local service providers for group rates/discounts?
- Form internal support networks unrelated to professional goals?
- Dedicate a private area of your office for personal use – nursing mother's room, emergency playroom, private phone room (for placing sensitive calls within an open workspace)?

HOW ARE THEY MANAGING IT?

POLICIES AND PERKS alone don't tell the whole story. For that you need to talk to parents in the trenches. During the many interviews I've conducted for this book and during my overall research on the generations, two things stand out as the harbingers of a family-friendly work environment: flexibility and accountability. One does not work without the other.

At EF Education First, a Boston-based worldwide education and cultural exchange organization, that philosophy starts at the top. A family-owned company, EF always has stressed the importance of developing a strong work-life balance and goes out of its way to support its parents and families. From the very beginning, the founder of the company created a family-oriented organization and he is now passing the business to the next generation. Because of its family environment, the company is supportive of the need to balance business and family and works with employees on an individual basis to figure out how to accomplish that.

Sherri Fletcher at Enterprise and Plante & Moran's Michelle Kolb agree: For effective family- and life-friendly policies and strategies to work, the company culture needs to embrace this attitude of viewing employees as whole beings. However, both point out that the best solutions often come from the staff level, where the demand is felt strongly. "Given the opportunity, we've found that employees are very creative, and really quite fair, when they recommend solutions for work-life balance," Fletcher said. "And it is important to remember that it can take a while to move a large corporation … everything takes time. But when leadership is open to change and employees are thoughtful in creating proposals that are win-win situations, it is amazing how the company culture can embrace new initiatives and make a real difference in the lives of its employees."

What stands out to me in that conversation, and hopefully you picked up on it too, is that leaders need to be willing to change. Sure, Manager A said he wanted things to be different, but that's a far cry from being willing to change oneself to make that difference come about. Through my travels and conversations with companies like Enterprise, I've become rather optimistic that change is possible in companies of any size as long as the leaders are open to it. *If everyone struggling with inertia could see what I've seen — that when Boomers and Matures give up a little of their "back in my day, gotta pay your dues" mentality and look at how to make things work with the Xer and Millennial cards they've been dealt, the younger generations return the loyalty and productivity in spades — I believe this generational gap would begin to dwindle exponentially.* It takes a true "give a little, gain a lot" mind-set and, as you'll keep seeing here, it works.

The conundrum lies, perhaps, in not wanting to give too much. Not wanting to lose control or the respect of your staff. That is where accountability comes in, an ongoing theme among all of these generationally driven changes.

Kelly Harrison is a nurse manager at a mid-Atlantic regional medical center and the mother of two. While nursing does have nontraditional shifts, which can be helpful to some parents' schedules, it does not allow for as much flexibility in the moment. For Harrison, the answer is to lead by example. She has several options in place for backup care in case one of her children misses school. In her management role, actual hours are not as stringent as they are for the nurses under her watch, however Harrison recognizes the bind they are in and wherever possible holds herself accountable to the same standards.

"Heart vs. handbook is always a challenge," she notes. "I'm a mother; I understand the conflict. But it is a numbers game and we must put patient care first."

In an attempt to control unscheduled absences and relieve the pressure to fill missed shifts, the hospital where Harrison works recently launched a "bid shift" initiative that allows managers to list open shifts and have nurses volunteer to work them in exchange for bonuses or increased overtime. This has encouraged employees to proactively plan their time away and offers a channel for managers to find qualified staff on short notice, as well as in advance.

While this is a challenge that is often created by Xers — as parents they are more frequently in position to need time off, both planned and unexpected — the bid shift solution is good for everyone. Harrison notes that Boomers and Millennials are the most likely to accept shift bids, surmising that this is because they have more flexibility in their schedules and/or more compelling financial demands. "My Boomer employees will pick up extra shifts to help pad their retirement funds, while the Millennials mention vacations and car purchases," she said. Bid shift functions beautifully because it taps into the notion of time as a currency, keeping control on the side of the employee while ultimately delivering committed workers where the hospital needs them.

TAKEAWAYS

Gaining responsibility for others – whether children or aging parents – means losing some control over schedules and life in general. Support workers facing increased personal responsibilities by marrying flexibility with accountability:

- Be clear about expectations – non-negotiables must be identified up front.
- Rethink your typical work schedule. Focus on end goals rather than traditional workplace routines.
- Create ways for employees to earn flexibility and/ or make up for unexpected absences.
- Hold everyone accountable for the non-negotiable items, regardless of flex arrangements – this minimizes resentment from coworkers
- Better yet, make flex benefits available to all who earn it through their productivity, not necessarily just for those with special circumstances
- Flexibility may always be revoked if accountability is not there. While flex arrangements are created to assist life balance, the work quality must hold.

As women continue to gain numbers in the workforce – in February 2010 women surpassed men in the nation's payroll for the first time in history, thanks largely to the recession[13] – the needs of the working parent must increasingly become part of the business conversation. It cannot be assumed that every family has a primary breadwinner and a primary homemaker. The needs of the family are entering the workforce in a way that is unprecedented. For better or for worse, it is the makeup of our workforce today, and for the foreseeable future. Creating an environment that allows parents to care and provide for their children while also maintaining productivity standards is likely to make the difference between those companies that get ahead and those that are left behind. Remember, today's employees learned that they work for themselves, not the company. However, they will be extremely loyal to a company that understands where employees' individual values lie. For many Xers, and a growing number of Millennials, that starts with family.

TO THINK ON...

• **MOST SMALL ORGANIZATIONS** don't have a pregnancy policy or a sick-child policy; they simply figure things out internally along the way. What would be the impact of creating something formal for your workplace? Would your employees embrace it? Would it have an impact on retention? How about recruiting new people?

• **IF YOU'RE A BABY BOOMER,** chances are your employees will begin having children at an older age than you did and those children will be reliant upon their parents longer than your kids were. What are the implications of this to your workplace?

• **WE ALL THINK WE'RE FLEXIBLE.** Even Manager A considered himself a flexible manager, but are we? Normal people like routines, and we tend to feel threatened and inconvenienced when our routine is involuntarily broken. So ask yourself, "Am I flexible from my employees' point of view?" What little changes can you make that may be a small inconvenience for you but would make you much more flexible from your employees' point of view.

• **WHEN FLEXIBILITY IS GRANTED,** accountability must be maintained. How can you get your staff and team involved in maintaining accountability so that you are not the only one holding people accountable?

CHAPTER FOUR

THE GEN X MANAGER

Tips for Managing Up and Down the Generational Spectrum

DESPITE A SHIFT AWAY from a traditional corporate ladder career path, individuals are still advancing in their careers and moving from staff to management. Time marches on and even if the path is not strictly linear, nontraditionalist Xers are older (and wiser? At least less cynical?) and now occupying management positions throughout companies and organizations in large numbers. How are they approaching this new authoritarian role? Does the traditional Boomer/Mature model emerge or do they work from a new playbook?

From numerous conversations through the years, I had my notion as to the answer, but wanted to talk to some Gen X managers and see how they felt about stepping up and becoming the boss. I'm happy to share that my presumption was right on track – Gen Xers as managers are still Xers at heart. Their "get out of my way and let me do my job" attitude seems to prevail, even in this changing dynamic. In other words, the job changes, but not the person.

However, the shoe is firmly on the other foot. As managers, most of the Xers I interviewed expressed a strong desire to get themselves out of the way, so that their employees can do their jobs. In essence, they are trying to be the manager they wanted. And yet, they are working toward the same goals as their Boomer counterparts and predecessors. They are, per usual, approaching it in a slightly different way. A more informal structure often comes into play. *Accountability resurfaces, becoming more prominent as face time recedes.* According to the Gen X manager, if we are going to relax some rules, we need to hold one another responsible.

Another dynamic of Xers in management is that there continue to be a large number of Boomers in the workplace. And with economic trends indicating the potential for delayed retirements, this means many Xers find themselves managing up the generational chain. This can present some difficulty in meeting a variety of communication and leadership expectations.

Gen X managers will do well to apply their "get it done" attitude to this leadership role as well – understanding that there is no one-size-fits-all approach to motivating a team. What are some tricks of the trade that can help Xers thrive in these management roles? So glad you asked.

BECOME BOTH ACCOUNTABLE AND ACCESSIBLE

DURING THE INTERVIEWS conducted for this book, the Gen X managers I spoke with could well have been reading from a prepared script – and no, I didn't send them one. I talked to nurse managers, hospital administrators, financial planners, dot-com entrepreneurs, education innovators, travel experts and more. To the one, each shared a strong message of personal responsibility and accountability. All eschewed the notion of micromanagement:

- "You have a job; here are the expectations, figure out how to make it work."
- "You are responsible for X; I don't care how you do it, just make sure it happens,"
- "Here is the desired result, get us there."
- "Respect the job, respect yourself, and be fair with your time."

At first blush this seems like a fine managerial trait – treat everyone like responsible adults and expect them to pull through. And it is a fine trait ... to a point. The Gen X manager has to make certain that this hands-off management style doesn't warp into a disconnected one because not every employee is equally self-motivated and -directed.

Andrew Weber, a hospital administrator for the mid-Atlantic medical center mentioned in Chapter Three, makes certain that his door is always open for staff seeking to share an idea or get some advice. And he means physically open – a "come to me any time" philosophy is quickly negated if the door is a physical barrier to entry. This allows Weber's team access to him for quick check-ins that meet the employee's needs, whether that is a Boomer's desire for a little face time or a Millennial's need to make sure he's on the right track with an assignment. The open-door policy signifies trust, availability and that the employee's time is as important as the boss's. The open door policy is by no means a new management characteristic, but it still speaks volumes about a manager and how accessible he or she is.

The line between micromanagement and support is rather thin. Weber's colleague, Kristi Snyder, recognized this in her own management habits. "I struggle with balancing face time – which is very much desired by my Boomer staff members – and my Xer desire to 'get it done' regarding my *own* work tasks" she notes. "It would be easy to stay in my office all day – there is certainly enough work! But I realize that it is important to get out there and make connections with the staff and other managers. I will admit that is something I have to make a conscious decision to work on."

While all Generation Xers will not be the same, they are largely nomads when it comes to their workplace. They want to come to work, get their work done, and go. Face time isn't something they particularly want or need. And their lives are still defined by who they are outside of work, not the job. That part of them remains unchanged. Early on they found the quickest way to accomplish this was to keep their heads low and engage with their peers only when necessary. They aren't rude or mean; they are simply not as social as the Boomers, at least not in the same way. It's the latchkey kid in the workplace. The latchkey kid got home from school and had chores to do at home while they were alone and Mom and Dad were working. This ethic is now visible in the workplace – get to work, get it done, and keep to yourself. The Boomers, however, are very different, which has created challenges as Xers join the management ranks.

Boomers need, want and, indeed, expect face time. This can be difficult for Gen X managers who are happy to work in a more isolated environment. While the Xer wants to know the expectations and be allowed to go off into his own world to fulfill them, the Boomer needs more frequent contact with the team. Managers need to find that balance and Xer managers must step outside their comfort zone to meet the face-time needs of Boomer reports if they are to get results. The Xer manager may find this burdensome or even a bad use of time. But Boomers *need* face time. They build consensus in person and reaffirm the goals of what they're doing. Boomers also tend to want very clear instructions. They'll ask, "What, exactly, are you looking for so I can do my best to deliver the first time?" Team players to the end, they want to be working toward a well-defined company goal.

The inverse can be a problem, too. When a Boomer is managing an Xer, that Boomer manager may seek lots of face time to build consensus and reaffirm the goal and the mission. The Boomer manager may get frustrated that the Xers are not motivated by this face time and team-building process. What the Boomer calls face time and productive consensus building, the Xer will often perceive as micromanagement. *As a manager it is important to give the guidance that is needed and desired by the employee, which is not always the guidance or the approach that you would want if roles were reversed.* This is one case where the Golden Rule can use a little tweaking.

Millennials, too, require some guidance in order to perform as desired. Laura Lashbrook is director of training and development at Clarity, a Gen X-owned boutique staffing firm with offices in New York, San Francisco and Palo Alto. Lashbrook noted that Millennial workers do best when managers create some structure around performance and expectation management. Unlike many Xers, Millennials like having some set guidelines and parameters in order to succeed. Lashbrook mentions that "they respond to positive reward, but don't necessarily solicit feedback or help as often as others. They need to be prompted or have space made to allow for specific guidance."

To accommodate this need, Lashbrook has biweekly meetings in which each employee is responsible for coming with goals, examples of successes and areas in which they want to improve. This structure creates a framework where everyone contributes and is given an opportunity to receive not only needed help, but plenty of positive feedback as well.

In doing this, Lashbrook brings up another key point to managing the Millennials. Because of their somewhat coddled childhoods, they need to hear loads of positive feedback. Perhaps more than you are used to giving, or even comfortable offering at first. Remember the whole "trophy for participation" concept? Positive reinforcement for doing the basics of the job at hand is the workplace equivalent. This generation needs both validation that they are successfully completing the job, and then additional reward for going above and beyond. Yes, it is an extra step for you, but it pays off.

TAKEAWAYS

Holding others, and yourself, accountable speaks to trust and respect – both highly valued through the generations. Demonstrating these traits is not something that can be easily turned on or off, but there are broad-range strategies that can help keep accountability consistent.

- Honor commitments. Expect others to honor theirs.
- Apply consequences/make amends when a situation falls short. For example, suspend flex schedule offerings for employees who cannot meet obligations, or offer additional PTO when a meeting requires attendance outside of an agreed flex schedule.
- Enforce schedules – both the time on and the time off. If there is a suggested maximum hours per week, make sure employees honor it to avoid burnout.
- Create opportunities for check-ins – seek employees out if they don't touch base on occasion; don't expect they will always come to you.
- Match check-in style to individual employee preferences – e-mail, in person, phone, even text. Communicate in their preferred manner, which may not always be yours.

INTERESTED BOSS OR INVOLVED FRIEND?

IF MAKING CONNECTIONS with the team is important to establishing leadership, wouldn't becoming buddies be even better? What about those situations where you are promoted to managing your current peers, the ones with whom you already socialize? Even easier, right? Not quite. As Kelly Harrison sums it up, "my job is not to be friends, but to be responsible." While the two are not mutually exclusive, putting parameters on social relationships with staff is crucial. Yet, as we'll discuss in more detail later on, the social needs of some generations, especially Millennials, run very strong. So proper balance is key.

This can be a tricky territory for those who move from staff to managing their peers, and it is an especially important distinction with Millennial staff who often desire personal connections at all levels of the organization.

With 50 percent of his team on the Millennial end of the spectrum, David Houchins sees the social dynamic very clearly every day. And while he enjoys a tremendous rapport with his team, he never partakes in purely social activities. "They ask all the time, but I am always conveniently busy," Houchins jokes. "They've probably noticed by now that I never come, but they always ask. I'm not sure if it's just a routine at this stage or if the offer itself is important to their desire to be inclusive, but there are certainly no hard feelings amongst us."

Houchins does make very strategic use of social occasions, however. He ties them to professional goals. He has built numerous social activities into performance awards – with monthly and quarterly opportunities to score dinner with the boss, for example. Recently he created an even larger incentive – meet half-yearly goals and the whole group will do something together. The team, which comprises eight Millennials, five Xers and four Boomers, chose to embark on a three-day cruise. The time off is excused by the agency, but each team member will pay his own way – the team decided this collective time off for socializing and celebrating would be worth it.

Andrew Weber agrees with Houchins. As a hospital administrator, Weber always has work-related social activities on his schedule. But every charity dinner, physician breakfast and recruitment event has a decidedly professional purpose – there is no socializing just for fun.

Bear in mind, the Millennial generation has had coaches, troop leaders, and even parents who have acted more like "friends" than bosses or leaders. "Quality time" became the cry of parents everywhere and, in many cases, its introduction to the household dynamic sent discipline and traditional models of leadership packing.

In fact, Millennials have experienced relationships that are more like friendships with most of the older people they've interacted with throughout their lives. Many parents, coaches and teachers have all judged success on how well-liked they were. It sounds ridiculous when stated plainly, but it rings true, doesn't it? So when Millennials seek that same type of relationship with you – and you don't embrace it or even push it away – it is an unfamiliar response, which may leave them a bit taken aback and, possibly even offended. You need to let them know that you care about them, that you want them to succeed, and that *you're here to help but that you serve a different role than friend*. It can be hard to do, but it is very important.

Why is it so important? It's simply too easy to let personal friendships muddy the professional waters, especially in the more informal environments that Gen X managers prefer. If you find yourself moving from concerned boss to de facto psychiatrist or drinking buddy, it's time to re-evaluate and set clear boundaries.

TAKE AWAYS

Despite changing work habits, the team is still important. Protect and encourage your relationship with the team by retaining interest in the person while respecting the boundaries of the boss/employee relationship. This can be especially difficult when your direct reports are also same age peers. To find that comfortable middle ground:

- Keep purely social interactions within the regular work day – grab lunch instead of an after-hours drink, for example.
- Make outside events clearly professional – client dinner, company banquet, etc.
- Consider the audience – if nonemployees are in attendance (friends, spouses), then that is a pretty good indication of a purely social event.
- Be consistent – a friend to all but a buddy to none.

INVITE COMMENTARY, ENCOURAGE INVOLVEMENT

SO WE'VE TALKED ABOUT the fact that Gen X managers tend to prefer a hands-off approach, but need to stay connected. Then we told you to be mindful of socializing if there is no distinct professional purpose. Seems like the proverbial spot between a rock and a hard place. How are you supposed to get connected if you aren't supposed to socialize?

That's where Weber's open-door policy comes into play. Being a good listener is one of the most important managerial traits in general, and it becomes even more so when the manager in question is working with the expectations of a variety of generations. Truly listening and valuing employee views will pay tremendous dividends.

If opening yourself or your management to conversation is not natural for you, perhaps some of these approaches will help facilitate more interaction.

At Strategic Financial Group, a MassMutual general agency, the Millennials on David Houchins' team are actively involved in recruiting. In fact, a team of five once invited themselves on a campus recruiting outing and ended up having one of the most successful events in the team's history. Not only did the team members get to have stronger say in who was called back after interviews, but the recruits also were able to get highly valued peer-to-peer reviews on what it is really like to be part of the MassMutual family. As a result, the follow-up interview and offer process was streamlined to include those individuals who had been pre-vetted by the team and therefore more likely to be genuinely interested in the position as well as more apt to be a good fit for the culture.

Employee input is critical to success. A New England online company relies on an open hiring process, including peer reviews, to make certain that everyone fits the company culture before they even join. A hospital in the heartland involves employees in the interview process to make sure candidates are a good fit for the team. As a hospital administrator told me, "In our environment we work together and interact together all the time. When we need a new person we tell our staff that they'll be involved in selecting this person and they need to 'pick their family.' It seems to work because we have very few miss-hires."

One company I checked with holds regular town hall style company meetings in which employees are encouraged to ask questions and provide feedback on specific topics. Participation is expected. Not only does this setting provide ample opportunity for the CEO to take the pulse of the employees, but it also helps the entire staff openly discuss issues that are or will be important to their daily work environment.

RANKS OFF MEETINGS

SCOTT KLOSOSKY IS a technology entrepreneur and business consultant who has launched numerous successful businesses and helps business leaders take a "future point of view" for their companies. A few years back he began implementing "Ranks Off Meetings" at his companies, a strategy he first learned from Leland Russell, co-author of *Winning in FastTime*.

The Ranks Off meeting is an outgrowth of a strategy employed by a military leader who was faced with the daunting task of ending a conflict in three short weeks. This Air Force colonel brought together 100 people from all branches and levels of the armed forces to brainstorm a solution. Rank patches were literally taken off and left at the door – inside the room no one person had seniority or authority over another. Everyone brought a unique perspective to the conversation and all ideas were valued.

"This concept works brilliantly in the business world," Klososky states. "It doesn't matter what rank you are, but how powerful your ideas are. Leaders are often surprised at just how insightful staff can be given a specific problem to solve."

This is music to the Millennial and Xer ear. "They think they have great ideas and need a forum to express them," Klososky reflects.

The desire to belong, to be important, and to not work for work's sake is huge among the younger generations at work today. Ranks Off meetings appeal to that go-getter, antihierarchal attitude. They let the "little people" have a taste of power. And that taste not only keeps them committed, but it also helps bring about even greater solutions for the company.

To be sure, Ranks Off meetings require some ground rules to be effective. In his experience, Klososky has determined that in order to deliver results the meetings must:

- Be official.
- Have full buy-in from top leadership.
- Address a specific problem.

In practice, it is also important that there be a culture of trust throughout the organization. Klososky recognizes that a Ranks Off meeting can be a challenge for companies that are not used to consensus building or that shy away from opening management conversations to the rank and file. However, he is confident that when the process is trusted and managers seek out the opinions of others – even putting them on the spot if someone needs to get the ball rolling – the result is greater than if management is left to make decisions in the privacy of the boardroom. In fact, *he estimates that a Ranks Off meeting generates a 25 percent better solution than if management handled things alone.* Why is that? Detailed, in-the-trenches experience adds depth to the end result. And those details come from the rank-and-file workers who are often Xers and Millennials – generations that want to have their say and make their work lives easier at the same time. Talk about perfect conditions.

Taking the current budget crisis as an example, Klososky offers a hypothetical example where a company needs to slash the budget by 20 percent. Standard operating procedure is for the executive team to identify certain positions and functions for layoffs. One cut, problem solved. In a Ranks Off meeting, however, the 20 percent cost reduction may be found by fine-tuning numerous line items and saving more jobs. The folks in the trenches know where the daily fat is and, given the chance, can be creative in significantly reducing overhead while still achieving company goals and minimizing layoffs. And when layoffs are required, they can often identify the most effective ways to redistribute that workload without overburdening any one area or employee. In short, the collective thinking of a Ranks Off meeting can yield a more precise and efficient solution to the same problem, simply because greater real-world detail is taken into consideration.

When properly executed, Ranks Off meetings can permeate the culture of an organization. They signify that everyone has value and everyone will be heard. This is an empowering message for your people, and it helps build trust and loyalty in the organization, something that is notably lacking in this generation.

Klososky shares how the Ranks Off meeting has impacted his management style: "My companies have a 'no secrets' rule – you can ask any question of any person at any time and you must get an answer. The only exception is payroll.

This provides a transparency that keeps leadership on their game and demonstrates the value of every employee."

Trust is a two-way street. Klososky reports that it takes about six months for people to become comfortable with this open communication, but ultimately they can see how empowering it is and how the quality of ideas improves. If your company is hesitant to share more information or include more people in brainstorming solutions, take it one step at a time. Introduce Ranks Off meetings for smaller-impact discussions to gain comfort with the concept. Ultimately, executives want to succeed. The proof will be in the results of those first meetings. And you can grow from there.

TAKEAWAYS

Keeping employees informed – and even included in the decision-making process – on subjects traditionally outside their job parameters is a great way to demonstrate their value and to encourage them to know and care more about the company as a whole. It also fosters loyalty to those leaders willing to open up, and as loyalty to the individual outranks company loyalty as a retention incentive, the benefits are clear. There are many ways to be inclusive.

- Broadcast board meetings or make minutes available to all employees.
- Involve peers in the hiring process – include them in the recruitment teams and interviews; pair them with new recruits for first-day/week orientation
- Hold regular town hall meetings for the group and/or company, providing a frequent, open forum for communication.
- Approach specific problems with a Ranks Off meeting or a cross-function task force.
- Demonstrate value by seeking out and respecting viewpoints throughout all levels of the organization.
- Make inclusiveness part of the company culture – embraced by leadership and executed by all. If this is new, take baby steps until everyone is comfortable and authentic.

TO THINK ON...

• **ARE YOU A GEN X MANAGER?** If so, and if you fit the Gen X profile, chances are you avoid face time. You do it when you have to but you don't seek it or embrace it. To be successful in your career you MUST get comfortable with face time. Boomers and Millennials like it, and they will be the key to your management success. Bottom line: Get used to it.

• **HOW CAN YOU TRY** a Ranks Off meeting to solve a specific problem? How can you simply stick your toe in the water and give it a go?

• **AS THE HOSPITAL** administrator said, "Pick your family." How can you get your employees involved in "picking their family" to reduce miss-hires and giving your employees some ownership over finding a good fit for their team?

• **ARE THERE EMPLOYEES** who you might consider your friend? Is this a workplace hazard? How can you shift these dangerous relationships so that the company's success and your friendships don't become mutually exclusive at some point down the road?

CHAPTER FIVE

COMMUNICATION COMMUNICATION COMMUNICATION

Why Is Talking to Each Other So Difficult and Can We Make It Any Easier?

SPEND JUST A FEW moments speaking to a room full of employees and Millennials will be quite easy to identify. Not just by their youth and attire, but by their habits. They will be sitting together, probably texting while you talk, and eager to move on to the next subject. You may think they are rude beyond measure and not paying attention to a thing you say, as we saw with David Houchins' team at the opening of this book. And while that may occasionally be the case, quite frequently they will be the ones most likely to come up after the conversation to ask follow-up questions or continue the dialogue via e-mail in the next several days. They are paying attention; they simply have a different way of looking at the world and of working within it.

It bears reminding that Millennials have been raised in a world of constant entertainment, information and interruption. Ever connected by technology, they are multitaskers to the nth degree – they even Tweet in church. And while your mind may not be programmed to process that way of thinking, it is their way. For Millennials, texting while listening isn't rude, it's effective. We can debate that until the cows come home, but the truth is that this generation does both. In fact, they often need to do both in order to do either well. In a way, multitasking keeps them in the game.

While the Millennials are huddled together Tweeting, Boomers and Xers are working out some communication idiosyncrasies of their own. Most notable is the Xer penchant for being direct — occasionally to the detriment of common courtesy. Once again, the *intent* of the outspoken Xer is usually not to be discourteous, but rather to eliminate unnecessary time and energy spent sugarcoating to make concerns, complaints and observations more palatable. They just want to say their truth and get back to work. Boomers in the meantime are calling meetings to hash out issues that Xers believe can be handled in a quick e-mail.

In short, everybody's talking, but nobody's hearing each other. The fix is in both understanding communication styles and deciphering generational definitions. As I've mentioned, each generation has its own definition of some basic business and personal values. Like the old-fashioned game of telephone, where one person whispers a sentence to the next and so on through a line until the last person restates the sentence as a jumbled mess, generational definitions can distort the meaning of a seemingly innocent conversation and leave all participants frustrated.

This quick and dirty generational dictionary illustrates the effects generational perspective can have on even the simplest of communications.

	MATURE	BOOMER	XER	MILLENNIAL
TIME	Company owns it	Company owns it	Mine, will rent	Let's barter
LOYALTY	To the company	To the job	To the leader	To my peers
SACRIFICE	Life	Liberty	Time	Convenience
TECHNOLOGY	Space shuttle	Television	PC	iPod apps
RESPECT	Expected	Given	Earned	Earned
MANAGEMENT	Authority	Leader	Nuisance	Guide
MUSIC	Radio	Record Shop	CDs	Download
FACE TIME	What?	Powerful	Pathetic	Social
ADULT	16	18	21	30
TITLES	Respected	Impressive	Empty	Irrelevant

So you can see that many of the same words have completely different meanings depending on who is saying them and who is hearing them. It makes sense, then, that when a Boomer boss asks his employees to work on Saturday, the Matures and Boomers agree, while the Xer thinks about it and the Millennial asks what he'll get in exchange. *There is a fundamental difference between the generations in the assumption of who owns that time.* Remembering this and making sure that everyone has a mutual understanding of expectations will go a long way toward improving the communication among a generationally diverse team.

A NEW BRAND OF FACE TIME

XERS ARE OPENLY abhorrent of clocking in for the sake of face time. Whether that is because they view the workday as more fluid or because they want to be able to benefit from their own time management efficiencies, they see no reason to be visible for visibility's sake. Yet they do want the promotion opportunities that come with being recognized for a job well done. Millennials, likewise, aren't fans of old-school face time, but they do strongly value the social aspect of getting in front of their workplace peers. In a team environment, they still want to check in with each other and with the boss.

David Houchins conducts weekly one-on-one accountability meetings with each salesperson on his Strategic Financial Group team. Each of these meetings lasts roughly 30-50 minutes depending on the needs of the individual. Newer team members get 50 minutes a week, while those who are more established may only need to connect for 30 minutes every week or two. It's easy to see that with a growing sales force, manager Houchins faces the incredibly shrinking workweek – at least as it pertains to time available to focus on his own work tasks. However, he asserts that *the connections created are well worth the time expended and that his team has come to rely upon this one-on-one time.* Not only does it provide an opportunity to give and receive individualized feedback, Houchins believes that these meetings demonstrate the importance of each individual to the team as a whole.

Houchins knows that when he can help his team members achieve their goals they will, in return, help him reach his own goals. This comes in handy, especially when in a pinch and needing to ask for that extra 110 percent. Houchins understands the value of "chips" and gives them freely knowing that his team will be eager to help when the time comes to cash them in.

"My team knows I've got a busy workload and diligently balance my home and professional lives," he explains. "So when they see me dedicate nearly 50 percent of my workweek to their individual success, it speaks volumes. My team knows I am committed to them and, as a result, they are excruciatingly loyal to me."

At these weekly check-ins, they sit down and talk about upcoming challenges and opportunities, review past successes and failures, and generally spend a few moments touching base. Houchins is able to offer advice pertinent to specific current challenges and the employee is able to request insight in a nonthreatening environment or get personalized kudos for a recent business win. It is a time to reaffirm and realign.

If your team is too large or dispersed for weekly meetings, consider a biweekly sit-down or phone call. There are numerous ways that face time can manifest based on the realities of your work environment. The one constant is that managers dedicate regular blocks of time to giving employees individualized attention and that the communication highway is open in both directions.

SIT DOWN FOR A LITTLE KISS-KICK-KISS

THERE ARE SOME specific communication tactics that can help managers deliver their intended message and improve the likelihood of getting the intended result. Since we've been talking about meetings, let's jump right into the subject of disciplinary conversations. With their youth filled with coddling and de facto self-esteem training, the younger generations today are clearly not prepared for a dressing down by the boss. Being called out for a poorly executed task does not embarrass them into shape; it simply makes them lose all respect and interest in the boss and pushes one foot out the door.

So how can you communicate a need for improvement or convey dissatisfaction without sending them running to their parents (don't laugh, it happens). Use what I like to call the Kiss-Kick-Kiss principle. That is, compliment whatever is going right, mention the problem at hand, and then close with an upbeat message about working through this together. Whoa! Slow down. Manager A is having a fit right about now, isn't he? Why is it your job to help them do their job better? Well, because ultimately you want the job done better, right?

The Millennials need that guidance. They need the support that says, "we will make this work." *Cushioning your criticism with praise on one side and support on the other will allow your employee to hear your message, save face, and exit the uncomfortable conversation with a plan for how to avoid this situation in the future.* Where possible in the conversation, ask the offender to give you an explanation of their behavior. But do not engage in an argument about the validity of that explanation.

It takes a little more time on the front end, and a little more self-control, but the result is that your employee is able to retain his or her connection with the boss, and today that equals loyalty to the company.

One more thing on the Kiss-Kick-Kiss principle: Be careful to not include any emotion in your conversation, nor assertions of emotion. For example, don't say "you got mad" or "you got lazy" or "you're unhappy with your assignment." Nothing emotional at all. Simply cite exactly what you've seen and whatever grievance has been documented. Only facts, no assumptions.

It is also worth noting that some youths today have found themselves in positions of leadership and they need to learn to give corrective feedback to their teams, which often have members who are older than they are. A Millennial dressing down a Boomer, or even Xer, is an awkward situation as it is important to learn an easy way to do it without too much discomfort from either side.

One additional benefit to the Kiss-Kick-Kiss Principle is that it is a super way to "manage up." Giving feedback to your boss in this format is often a way to make sure he/she knows what you like and what you do well but what has not been working for you lately. You finish with a suggestion of some things that you and he/she can change to get you back into the zone, and you've effectively told your boss what is needed to get you working hard again.

Truth be told, all generations would love to be treated this way. They don't all require it like Millennials seem to, but Kiss-Kick-Kiss is a simple approach to implementing corrective measures and protecting relationships at the same time

TEACHING REAL MARKET VALUE

ALONG WITH YOUNGER employees' healthy self-esteem, you may have also noticed an inflated, or to be more precise, *inaccurate*, sense of personal value. In short, they don't think they are paid enough. We may think, well, who does? But the truth is that young workers simply do not have the perspective to understand their total cost of employment. Once again, you can't hold people accountable for what they've never been taught. So, along with time management, it is a good idea to do some educating on their personal market value.

Every employee is acutely aware of his or her salary or wage, but many are unaware of their true cost of employment. Begin the conversation by writing out on paper the employee's salary or a round number close to their salary (round low vs. high). Then increase that number by 30 to 50 percent (multiply by 1.3 to 1.5). That is the true cost of employing that individual.

That number now includes not only salary but all the other costs borne by an employer:

- Health insurance.
- Unemployment taxes/insurance.
- Retirement contributions and plan management.
- Heating, cooling, lighting, telephone service, etc. for the office.
- Computer equipment, maintenance, and software licenses.
- General business supplies – paper, copiers, etc.
- Any workplace perks
- Break room supplies, water service, and much more.

Most employees are unaware that their true cost of employment is that high, and only consider the amount of their salary when figuring their cost. The truth is much different.

Continue the conversation by talking about the value of the employee to the organization. Raises are granted for those who are more valuable than their cost. In other words, they earn more for the company than what they cost. Much of these earning are not measurable in terms of dollars. They're measurable in terms of arriving to work on time, chipping in to help the team, learning more about one's job to become more valuable to the team and at the workplace, being a good team member, being easy to work with and having a positive attitude. Raises aren't granted for being in the job for a certain time period; they're granted to those who produce greater value than what they've been paid.

Similarly, employees who are breaking even – only as valuable as what they are paid – can expect to remain in the same position for the foreseeable future. And when times get tough, these employees are likely the first to be cut. When an employee becomes less valuable than his cost of employment, his likelihood of being fired increases tremendously.

To put it in numbers...
New Sales Hire starting salary: $44,000
True cost of employment ($44,000 x 1.5): $66,000

This person can ask for a raise when she's confident her *value* to the workplace is greater than $66,000. To add to her value she can show up on time, work well within her team, accept roles of responsibility when asked, learn all she can about her job, offer to help out when not asked, and do the job well and thoroughly.

This person risks being let go when her *value* is $66,000 or below. An employee decreases her value when she is habitually late, misses deadlines, needs extra attention from supervisors, does only the minimal amounts needed to get the job done, or exhibits a negative attitude.

Make certain your employees understand their true cost of employment, as well as their current real market value to the company. And when discrepancies arise, use Kiss-Kick-Kiss to come up with a plan of action that will set them back on the right path.

DEALING WITH "WHY?"

AS XER AND MILLENNIAL generations postpone adulthood beyond the traditional boundaries of high school or college graduation, they hold on to some of the trappings of youth, for better or for worse. One of the unanticipated results of this new "adultolescence" life stage is the stretching of seemingly childlike attitudes, notably the use of the word "why."

Back in the days when children were meant to be neither seen nor heard, "why" was a short-lived communication of toddlers and teens. Why? Because I said so. Today, "why" has a legitimate place in the conversation of younger generations. Not only do they question authority based on the deteriorating value of institutional leadership in society as a whole, but their parents encouraged this behavior under the heading of "curiosity." They have simply become accustomed to asking the questions that are on their minds. They want to understand why they are asked to do something before they go do it. And therein lies the frustration for folks like Manager A who don't feel obligated to provide any further reason than because they did, indeed, say so.

The key to not being driven mad by the why is twofold – the understanding and the approach. First, understand that 97 percent of the time employees ask "why?" it is because they truly want to know the answer. They are curious as to how a solution or policy came about. They want to know the thinking behind the action. It is simply an inquiry, not a challenge. They gain value in knowledge, and they intend to follow the instruction, but they want to learn more about it first. That is not necessarily such a bad thing.

On the flip side, you don't always have the time or the inclination to provide an answer, and sometimes the answer needs to be "I'm the boss, that's why." That is okay – on occasion. Be careful how often you reach for that reply lest you risk alienating employees and losing that coveted loyalty. Remember, they want to feel a part of something bigger. They want to be valued for their ideas; and in order to learn how those ideas work in the company they need to learn how your ideas work. So explain.

Just as a question is not always a challenge, an explanation is not a deferment. The old school thinking of "I don't have to explain myself to you" is only true to a point. *You don't have to explain yourself with the expectation that the employee will grant permission, but you should be willing to teach what you know.*

So I challenge every manager out there to view "why" not as an affront to your leadership but as an opportunity to demonstrate it. Your blood pressure will thank you and you may just find that these nagging youngsters take your information and turn it into powerful new ideas.

A LITTLE MORE ABOUT RESPECT

IT SEEMS THAT everywhere I turn the laments come back to an underlying concern about respect. There is a frustration that because younger employees don't want to follow the same paths or offer blind obedience that there is an inherent disrespect for authority. Considering the reality that during the 2008 elections many conversations about possibility having a female president or vice president centered on whether their husbands would be referred to as "First Dude," this is not such a far-fetched concern. The definition of respect is undoubtedly shifting.

However, taking a generational perspective is once again imperative. The Xer and Millennial generations grew up in an era where institutional authority failed them at every turn – church scandal, presidential scandal, CEO corruption. You name it, it crumbled. And that is just on a macro level. Drill down to the home front and you have grandparents who don't want to be called grandparents because that sounds too old, fathers who don't want to be called Mr. Jones because "that's my father's name" and you quickly see how youths are being shown that age and experience don't necessarily equate to authority and respect. Even when respect exists, the language is shifting.

As we discussed early on, it's all in how you look at it. In fact, the lack of blind reverence to authority can have positive implications, too. A talent acquisition manager at a regional telecom company told me that while younger employees don't worry about titles, there is growing benefit to that viewpoint.

"I've noticed that the younger generations are not at all title-sensitive," the manager shared. "Our young Millennial intern, for example, is willing to talk to anyone, ask questions, and give input. It is not done in a disrespectful way; it is just more independent and assertive than many of the older generations who seem more intimidated by titles and place higher value on formality."

That last comment hits the nail on the head. Generally speaking, this holds true: The younger the individual, the more informal their communication style. This is why new staff members are comfortable addressing the CEO as "Joe" while tenured employees are often hesitant to speak to him at all, much less address him as "Mr. Smith."

It is a style, not a symbol. Informal is not always better, but it is much more comfortable for younger generations. Let it be if you can. *Remember to look at intent — is the lack of formality intentionally disrespectful or is it simply assertive or maybe just different?* Look with an open mind and the answer will be clear. With that said, if it is important to the company culture that a more formal communication style is adopted, follow Captain Ted's example: Make that expectation known and allow for a learning curve before holding them accountable to your new standard. And always, always, be prepared to answer "why?"

TAKEAWAYS

Communication is a two-way street, and that means sometimes adjusting your styles or preferences to those around you. The generations bring definitions, attitudes and logistical differences to the mix. You can't please everyone, but if you can keep the differences in mind it can impact how your messages are getting through.

- When possible, communicate in the style preferred by your audience, not yourself. This is usually in person for Boomers and Millennials and via e-mail for Xers. Disciplinary measures should always be taken in person.
- Remember differing definitions and spell out your expectations.
- Kiss-kick-kiss: Two positives for every negative.
- Let go of formality — or explain where it is expected and why.
- Ask for lots of feedback

TO THINK ON...

• AS A MANAGER, one of your roles is to correct workplace behavior as needed. How are you doing this? Is it in a way that motivated the offending employee to improve? Or in a manner that removes the employees' motivation? When a customer experiences poor service, it creates a big opportunity to fix the service in such a way that the customer is overwhelmed and becomes a loyal customer. The same is true with employee mistakes – it is a big opportunity to change the behavior and at the same time make a loyal and motivated employee. Use these opportunities wisely.

• BE HONEST WITH YOURSELF – how much do you cost to employ? Are you worth it? How can you become more valuable than your cost of employment? Might this be a good way to set an example for those you lead?

CHAPTER SIX

THE WORKPLACE GOES YOGA

When You Bend, Energy Flows

THERE IS NO DOUBT that today's workforce wants more control. They are not content with doing things as they've always been done, just because they've always been done that way. And as we've just discussed, they have new definitions and values for many business standards – time, reward, success – with time being perhaps the most controversial, or at least the most fervent. This has been the case for a long while. These were the changes Generation X ushered into the workplace 20 years ago. At that time senior generations said, "They'll grow up and come around." They clearly have not "come around."

According to Xers and Millennials, they own their time – not the employer. The company is simply renting a portion of it, and the employee decides how much is available for lease. This is a drastic shift from prior generations, but it is a true-to-the-core reality that you cannot change. The ability to control their own time is paramount to young workers. They don't see time in a box. Having been raised in a 24/7 access world, they don't believe in self-imposed time restrictions. Why does the report have to get written at 10 a.m. when I feel more energized at 10 p.m.? As long as it gets done by the deadline, right?

This changing definition of time and commitment is important to understand in order to *appreciate* the younger generations' work ethic rather than wonder where it is. The good news is that this can be accomplished fairly easily. Let's look at how some managers and companies have adapted policies and implemented tactics to address the changing definition of time.

These companies have tapped into their inner Gumby and are stretching the perceived boundaries of the typical work day, schedule or environment to address the reality that in today's 24/7 world, time is increasingly fluid.

FLEXIBLE SCHEDULES

YOUNGER GENERATIONS have a pronounced desire to control their time – to own their lives. They watched their parents suffer under the old-school views that the company owned its employees and they are not about to let that level of soul-numbing loss of control take hold. As a result, they want to have a say in their individual schedules.

Of course, flextime is not entirely new. Businesses have been searching for the ideal flex-schedule solutions for more than a decade. What is new is that this expectation is happening at the entry level. Employees just out of school want to discuss their ideal hours before even accepting the job. This is a new frontier and businesses need to be ready with a plan of action.

Or inaction. While flexible scheduling to some degree is a near-universal desire of the younger generations, it is simply not practical in all fields, especially those that involve customer face time and demand set coverage. If the ideas presented here are simply impossible for your work environment, be prepared to clearly explain that reality to new recruits – no beating around it – and to look for alternative ways to honor their need to balance and maintain ownership over time. Transparency in communication is critical to engaging younger workers today. They simply do not have patience for pandering, politics or hidden agendas.

FLEXIBLE WORK WEEKS

WHEN WE TALK about controlling our time, minds immediately go to telecommuting or nontraditional schedules (early/late starts or four, 10-hour days) – arguably the most frequently discussed forms of flextime. Yet, there are nearly as many ways to introduce flexible schedules as there are companies. Perhaps one of the following methods will work for your company or business unit, or maybe it will spark an idea that will fit your distinct workplace needs.

The lunch buffet

For many employees, lunch is simply a quick break to refuel. A full hour is often overkill. At Gold Star Speakers Bureau, the time is not wasted. The company, based in Tucson, Arizona, offers its employees an array of lunch options – not in the foods they consume, but when they do so. Staff members may choose to take shorter lunch breaks and apply the combined balance of time elsewhere in the workweek, such as leaving early on Friday afternoons. This is a great example of formalizing choices that employees may already be adopting casually.

Gold Star employees make a conscious choice to streamline lunch in order to take the extra consolidated time off in a way that is more valuable to them personally. The company retains its 40 hours of productive work time by simply reframing the window of productivity. Each employee's flex schedule, including lunch break timing, is decided in advance and becomes that person's set schedule. This allows the office to maintain adequate staffing over time without reevaluating schedules weekly.

Because of the company's West Coast location and nationwide clientele, Gold Star tends to have quiet Friday afternoons. Consistently lighter coverage works and the owners are happy to man the office in exchange for increased employee satisfaction. Additionally, employees who still want the full lunch hour but also want the early leave on Friday can opt for an earlier start time to make up the complete work week. This also helps Gold Star have staff on hand earlier in the day for its East Coast clients. It's all about matching employee desire with company needs and finding a solution that fits both, even if it's not the most traditional approach.

"Since implementing the policy, every single employee has opted to revise their schedules and take advantage of one shorter work day each week," says

Andrea Gold, President. "Productivity has not dropped at all. In fact, if anything it has risen as now everyone knows they have some extra time to tend to personal needs during the traditional workweek and therefore are better able to focus on work while at the office."

Goal-driven schedules
David Houchins guides his agency's sales team based on overall goals, rather than specific timelines. In sales, face time doesn't matter — results do. Therefore Houchins manages with minimal mandatory time restraints. Instead of worrying about specific hours in the office or in the field, he measures quality of performance. The sales team is held accountable to a weekly staff meeting and a weekly manager-employee check-in. That's it.

"My team is highly motivated to succeed — for themselves, for me, and for each other," Houchins explains. "I coach them on how to manage their time and be effective in the field, then get out of the way and let them do that. Certainly if I see someone putting in minimal effort for minimal reward, we will have a discussion. But my experience has been that these young team members work hard when they are working, and they want the results. And then they want the time to enjoy those results. As long as the results keep coming, I can't fault them for that."

Michael Kitces, a financial adviser with Pinnacle Advisory Group and owner of Kitces.com, also manages a team that combines sales and support staff, with clearly different time restraints. Flex schedules don't work when someone has to be there to respond to client needs, right? Well, maybe the two are not mutually exclusive.

Kitces reports that when the flexible schedules became a regular part of the sales team culture, some unhappiness began to brew on the part of the support staff who were required to work traditional hours to be available for client response. Instead of dismissing the idea of flextime for this employee group, however, Pinnacle's management team appealed to their sense of fairness and natural tendency to look out for one another. In other words, the ball was put back in employees' court: Figure out how to work flexibility into the week and maintain the necessary coverage and you can have it. The planning was left to the group to figure out, and they were able to come to agreement on a fair division of labor. As a result, all members of the Pinnacle team are able to exercise some measure of control over their schedules.

The 6-5-4 Plan

The southeast region of Enterprise Rent-A-Car has hit on a new use of time as a motivator. Faced with employee complaints about the long hours and loss of flexibility that often comes with being promoted to branch management, Enterprise crafted a time management program that emphasizes flexibility, balance, cross-team cooperation, and cost savings – all while *improving* customer experience. Pretty amazing.

I first heard about the plan when it was newly implemented and recently checked back in with Sherri Fletcher, the woman who launched it, to learn more about where it started and how it has developed over the years.

"As a retail environment, our customer-facing staff has to maintain specific store hours. That's not negotiable. Increasingly, that meant longer work weeks for our manager-level staff and less personal time. It was costly both in terms of payroll and burnout," Fletcher said. "Enterprise tackled it on two fronts. First, we created a 49-hour workweek cutoff. Employees are simply not allowed to work more than 49 hours. Next, we built some flexibility into schedules at the management level."

When Enterprise managers have to work a Saturday shift, they receive a set number of flex hours to use that same week, at their discretion. Branch managers receive six hours, assistant managers get five, and management trainees get four – hence my reference to the "6-5-4 plan" in my talks on the subject. The company allows some freedom on when the time is taken. Though it does need to be used the same week as the Saturday schedule and cannot be redeemed during the busy hours of Monday morning and Friday afternoon, employees have the choice of leaving an hour early each day or taking it all at once, or otherwise splitting the flextime to fit their needs. Since it is given freely according to the monthly schedule, the resulting coverage needs are determined in advance making sure customer service expectations are met.

What drew me to the 6-5-4 plan as a great example was its simplicity, its focus on fairness, and its grass-roots origins. You see, this was not, and still is not, company policy. It is a management strategy employed where it is needed and where it works – proof that change is possible even within large organizations. In fact, thanks to the success of the 6-5-4 plan in the southeast, more and more Enterprise regions are implementing it every year.

Speaking of changing large corporations, I specifically wanted to know what kind of resistance the program met at the outset. Fletcher admitted that some of the old guard were skeptical that the schedules would work, but they soon learned that it did. Fletcher and her team launched the program with a few focus groups before attempting to clear the executive culture hurdle. As a result she was able to demonstrate that coverage was maintained, overall overtime costs were reduced, and employee morale skyrocketed. Who can say no to that?

"It did take some trial and error, as any new initiative will," Fletcher shared. "There were some holdouts in the beginning, managers who weren't sure it was possible or who were reluctant to honor the flex. But we resolved that by monitoring schedules for a while and helping the teams learn to rely on each other to share resources and be fair to everyone. As a result accountability has increased and everyone is honoring the promise."

"The 49-hour week and flex schedules were foreign concepts at Enterprise six or seven years ago," Fletcher continues. "Now it is part of our culture."

That is a noteworthy comment – flexibility can become part of the culture, even when it has not been the norm. Accountability is a huge enabler of flexibility. And investing time on the front end to look at creative ways to allow for flexibility while still getting the job done means you are more likely to find a sustainable solution that not only meets the needs of the younger generation of workers, but also achieves the overall goals of the company.

CONSIDER A POLICY-FREE POLICY

SOMETIMES THE ADOPTING of a specific flextime policy is, by its nature, inflexible. Every employee does not have the same time constraints and individual work-life balance needs. Often the best policy is to have no policy at all. Instead adopt a company culture that promotes defining individual schedules according to mutually agreed-upon goals.

EF Education First and Gold Star Speakers Bureau are at two ends of the spectrum – one a global organization with more than 3,000 full-time employees, the other a small, entrepreneurial outfit with fewer than 30 staff – yet both have embraced customized flex policies and made them work. The critical element is that employees understand the responsibilities of their positions and the goals of the organization, while the company recognizes the value of flexible schedules, whether that be telecommuting, nontraditional hours or a combination of both. Reduced hours – say 32-hour weeks instead of 40 – and job sharing are additional options for custom work schedules, with appropriate adjustments to compensation and benefits.

Flexible schedules are essentially customized employment contracts and should be treated as such with both sides held accountable. Don't promise someone a 7 a.m.-3 p.m. schedule and then schedule weekly staff meetings at 4:30. If you can't honor it, don't offer it. Repealing benefits or reneging on commitments is high on the list of reasons Xers and Millennials alike are wary of authority. But make the effort to meet individual needs and honor the agreed-upon solution and you will score enduring loyalty points. Flexible schedules can be more difficult to manage but the resulting loyalty, efficiency and productivity of your staff is usually worth the energy.

TAKEAWAYS

Flexible schedules can take many incarnations. Consider the customer demands of your business and the individual expectations of your employees, and then open your mind to creative solutions to meet them both. Better yet, put the responsibility of the solution on your employees – you may be surprised at what they come up with.

- Shorten lunch breaks for a shorter overall workweek.
- Enforce maximum workload for hourly workers, minimizing burnout and overtime.
- Consider reduced schedules with corresponding reduction in benefits.
- Designate flextime by team, rather than function – allow each team to work out a fair schedule.
- Honor flextime as a true commitment of the company.
- Periodically review flex schedules to make certain that the balance of individual and business goals is still achieving results – an effective plan must work in practice, not just in theory. Adjust as needed.

THE VACATION REWARD CARD

- "That's one hour of my life I'll never get back."
- "He's living on borrowed time"
- "Earn a free vacation for just 90 minutes of your time"

Time is a currency. Xers and Millennials didn't make this up, but more than any other generations, they bring this expectation to the workplace. So what better way to meet their demands on time control than by giving it back an hour at a time in return for a job well done?

A few years ago at an event in Pierre, South Dakota, a gentleman named Mike Kane shared with me one of the most valuable tools his company, Midwestern Mechanical, had stumbled upon: the Vacation Reward Card. He thought it was a great real-world example of the "time as currency" notion that I had just discussed. I was impressed by the idea and the application, so I circled back to get the full story about the vacation card and see how it was working today.

Midwestern Mechanical is a regional plumbing company with 145 employees. According to Kane, it all started when the top managers were looking at employee training and incentives and recognized that their main relationship with the employees is through the day-to-day boss, the foreman. "People work for or quit the foreman, not Midwestern Mechanical," Kane said. "We wanted to do everything we could to help our foremen become really strong and develop solid relationships and loyalty with their workers. So we created a special training program that started with discussions on how to discipline well. The next step was how to congratulate and reward. We realized the foremen had authority to do group perks, such as buying lunch or bringing in doughnuts, but what we wanted was to offer something that would allow them to specifically recognize the individual who goes above and beyond. The Vacation Reward Card, instant recognition, was born."

VACATION REWARD

I WAS CAUGHT DOING SOMETHING GOOD!

MIDWESTERN MECHANICAL, INC.

Good for 1 extra hour of vacation time

To redeem, turn in to payroll department.

Vision

Midwestern Mechanical, Inc. is dedicated to serving and protecting it's employees, customers and the general public with expert knowledge, quality workmanship and integrity throughout our Plumbing, Heating and Fire Protection Divisions.

Performance With Pride

The reward card is good for one hour of paid time off and is awarded for exceptional behavior, not simply for performing as expected. The team at Midwestern wanted to be sure that the card was valued, therefore it had to be handed out carefully but also given and honored freely. There is no cap on the number of cards distributed nor on the number any employee can earn, no limit on how long they can be held before cashing in. In fact, some employees never cash them in, preferring to display them on their toolboxes as a badge of honor (Boomers, of course).

You are probably wondering how it works. Who gets the cards? Who gives them out? Midwestern Mechanical provides the cards to all managers and front-line supervisors; however, individuals can be nominated by anyone in the company. A first-year apprentice, for example, can choose to thank someone for exceptional service simply by going to his supervisor and requesting a card. This hierarchy-free approach adds even more perceived value to the recognition. In fact, Midwestern Mechanical encourages employees to share the cards outside the company as well (general contractors, vendors, etc). They know that most will not honor it, but they want to get their employees in the habit of recognizing excellent behavior.

As a result, Vacation Reward Cards are popping up in unexpected places. Kane tells the story of an employee who gave a reward card to a waitress in addition to her regular tip. She handed it in to her boss who, in turn, called Midwestern and asked whether it was legit. Kane explained the program to the restaurant owner and the owner went on to honor the extra hour in the waitress's pay. It was somewhat of a "pay it forward" movement and a great example of how the value of time is universal.

Logistically it is easier to keep tabs on than one might expect. The earned PTO has no restrictions beyond normal vacation guidelines, namely that it is requested and approved in advance. Hourly workers have the option of using the cards to simply add an hour's pay to the paycheck. Talk about time equaling money.

In our follow-up conversation, I asked Kane about any pitfalls in the program and he was hard-pressed to find any. He mentioned that in the beginning they were afraid that with so few restrictions placed on the cards people might go hog-wild with them. In reality, he reports that everyone has been very responsible, which has allowed them to keep the program going for more than four years. *It also elevates the status of cardholders; as everyone knows they are earned through hard work and exceptional service, not handed out like candy.* Kane estimates that approximately 100 cards are distributed and redeemed each year.

Communicating the purpose behind such a reward card is critical to its success. The Midwestern Mechanical card is designed for day-to-day encouragement, not to be confused with formal reviews and promotions. It is just one tool in the toolbox. Further, its value as recognition for exceptional work must be maintained. It is not the only answer and should not be relied on for personal loyalty. Kane and his management team remind supervisors that they still need to communicate and provide personal feedback, including a simple thank you and a handshake.

CHOOSE YOUR PRIZE

ANOTHER WAY THAT COMPANIES can provide flexible solutions to employee demands is through an options-oriented reward system. I like to joke about the Lucite Wall of Fame common to many Boomer offices – any activity, certification, award is either made into a trophy or framed and hung on the wall … and we wonder where those participation trophies for preschool soccer teams originate. But I digress. The point is that Boomers tend to like their rewards to be visible, while Xers may prefer some extra time off and Millennials might rather have a catered lunch. Drilling even deeper, one Xer may cherish some time off while another values a restaurant certificate to take her significant other to dinner. Presenting a menu of reward options allows employees to select those which they, personally, value most. Of course, reward options in each category should have similar actual and perceived dollar values for the company and employees.

TAKEAWAYS

Time is a reward to be valued as much as, if not more than, money itself. There are several ways to use time as both incentive and reward, providing recognition in the form employees desire for achieving the goals desired by the company.

- Implement a vacation reward card program like the one at Midwestern Mechanical.
- Make time off an option for meeting challenging goals: "If we get to X, everyone gets a day off."
- Place minimal restrictions on the redemption of time-based rewards – to be a true currency it must be allowed to be spent freely.
- Offer choices.

PRIORITIZE LIFE

MANY MANAGERS VIEW the Millennial work ethic as suspect. Do the younger generations even have a work ethic? Of course they do. What many lack, however, is the experience and discipline to transfer their work ethic from the self-centric environment of home or college to the other-centered environment of the average workplace. Yes, they've had to be in class on time and assignments have deadlines, but outside of these few hours a day, they've had control over when and where they get the job done and how they spend 75 percent of their time.

When entering a professional work environment, Millennials, especially, may benefit from very direct expectation setting as well as time-management training. They need to be shown *how* to balance their own needs with those of the company. To use a coaching phrase, they often mistake activity for accomplishment.

Remember that many in this generation may have never held a job until they entered your workplace. Summer jobs were often replaced with theater camp or Outward Bound. *As a whole, Millennials have worked less upon entering the workforce with their first real job than any generation before them and are therefore often unfamiliar with how work works.* Subsequently, many managers have found that they must help these new employees structure their days in the beginning. Managers now need to teach not only the specifics of the job at hand, but also the fundamentals of the working world, including how to prioritize their days so that the most important items will be done the right way at the right time. Likewise, if you make it an early priority to teach these fundamentals, it makes it much easier to hold them accountable later on and will likely increase overall productivity, as David Houchins has learned.

New recruits to the MassMutual Strategic Financial Group sales team are led through a three-week-long boot camp, the first day of which focuses on how to manage time and prioritize their whole lives – not just the work-related activities. As a Gen Xer, Houchins wholeheartedly supports the idea of work-life balance. He also recognized early on that his newest team members had a tendency to either immerse themselves so intensely in work that they would quickly burn out or seemingly exploit the micromanagement-free style Houchins prefers by keeping irreverent hours and occasionally losing focus. The fix was a Day 1 lesson in time management.

"I firmly believe that a well-balanced team member is a good team member," Houchins says. "I know where my own priorities lie –and work is not at the head of the class. Work is important, certainly, but it is not the most important. So *I coach my team to schedule their weeks by starting with their family commitments and then fitting work around that.*" Yes, you read that right. Read it again, though, because it is important.

This may seem counterintuitive coming from management, but the result is often greater productivity. The key is defining family commitments, which changes for everyone. For a recent college grad, it may be a recreation league softball team or weekly meet-up with a social group. For young parents, commitments tend to revolve around children – PTA meetings, volunteering and extracurricular activities. Or it may be as simple as a nonnegotiable family dinner. The actual commitments don't matter; the fact that they are important to the employee makes them worthy.

Once the family commitments are firmly in the calendar, Houchins advises his team members to look at their daily/weekly/monthly goals and work them around the other commitments. While some might balk at such a backwards strategy, Houchins finds that productivity actually increases with his approach because team members spend less time fretting about how to fit it all in and become more efficient overall. Notice again that Houchins asks each individual to prioritize his or her personal commitments first and then schedule work around those commitments. This is almost the direct opposite of the traditional workplace thinking. The result? Houchins' team works their tails off for him because he "gets them." The productivity of an accommodating workplace will beat the productivity of an oppressive workplace any day.

Of course, each person needs to be honest about which commitments fall into the nonnegotiable category. Once again, appealing to this generation's sense of fairness works to your advantage.

"My team doesn't want to take advantage of me," Houchins explains. "But more so, they don't want to be taken advantage *of*. Coaching them on time management is a small investment of time up front that pays immense dividends as they know that I see and value their whole selves. In turn they respect me and the company enough to work hard when they are at work, knowing they have time carved out to play hard as well."

COMMUNITY SERVICE ON THE COMPANY DIME

PERHAPS A MORE ALTRUISTIC and less direct way to reward employees in their currency of choice is paid volunteer time off. The younger generations as a whole, Millennials especially, have a tendency to be more active in socially conscious pursuits. They gravitate toward altruistic efforts and are eager to make a difference. From making purchases that support specific causes to getting involved in a hands-on manner, Millennials are leading the charge in volunteerism and activism. Xers and Boomers are not far behind. Though their personal causes may be different, most individuals have a passion for bettering the world in a specific way. Allow time for your employees to fulfill that passion within the course of the regular work schedule and you demonstrate your company's commitment to the greater good as well as show appreciation of employees as individuals with interests outside the organization.

Paid volunteer time off (PVTO), like flex schedules, can take many forms. Some companies allow employees to accrue PVTO in the same manner as they do regular PTO – for every X number of hours worked, X hours of PVTO are earned. Others offer paid time off only for activities that are within the organizations' core areas of interest, aligning volunteer time with company values. Whatever the approach, compensating employees for time spent giving back can elevate an organization in the minds of its employees and the greater community.

Here are a variety of ways companies can structure volunteer benefits:

o Goals first, then freedom. With this approach employees must have clear, measurable goals, such as billable hours or completed sales. After these goals are met, the employee is free to use his remaining salaried time contributing to volunteer activities. This works best when measured against monthly goals, versus week by week.

o Volunteer reimbursements. Sometimes volunteer activity comes in fits and spurts and is not easily measured out in even doses each month. Using this approach, employees submit records for volunteer time already served. In return, they are awarded additional PTO hours according to the company volunteer time exchange rate. This approach allows employees to accrue PTO hours for volunteer time worked at their discretion.

o Team-building volunteerism. Still another option is to use company time for a groupwide volunteer effort. These are often best received when the original idea comes from the employees rather than from top down. If approved by management, planning can be done largely on company time and then the entire team works together on a specific volunteer effort. Charity home construction, food bank operations, local playground builds, etc. are all examples of one-shot, large impact activities that can give back to the community while bringing a team together.

At EF Education First, team-building volunteerism was recently supersized. One division of EF runs international educational tours for schools and other large groups. In a brainstorm on new product offerings, an employee suggested service trips as a way to merge wanderlust with altruism. EF decided to test the idea internally and organized a service trip to Guatemala, where they taught English and did craft projects with children in a local orphanage. Each of the company's product lines paid for two spots on the trip, offering them to deserving employees. In addition, several staffers elected to go on the trip as a personal volunteer-vacation, paying their own way. The result has been an annual service trip that is simultaneously a volunteer opportunity, employee benefit and new product pilot.

TAKEAWAYS

Support volunteerism, improve employee morale and achieve community outreach goals with a strong corporate volunteer policy. It's a win-win-win situation for the employee, the company and the community.

- Choose whether to align volunteer policies with company goals/values and industry initiatives or to allow employee freedom in selecting individual outreach.
- Consider various matching gift options.
    - o Match individual cash contributions with business funds
    - o Match individual cash contributions with equal-value product or service.
    - o Match individual time with corresponding paid time off (or portion of PTO).
    - o Match individual time with corresponding company volunteer time.
- Organize companywide outreach such as toy/coat/supply drives, adopt a family for the holidays, Habitat house builds, school tutors, etc.
- Make time available during the work week for volunteering – monthly, annually.
- Form a charitable giving committee to track volunteerism and promote a range of volunteer opportunities to the workforce.

TO THINK ON...

MOST PEOPLE THINK that they're flexible, kind, and generous people. What would your employees say about your flexibility? Are you working with them on flexibility or are you creating such tight parameters that there really is none?

REMEMBER, THERE IS nothing wrong with removing a person's flexible schedule if they're not performing to the degree the two of you agreed upon at the start. It is hard; it is confrontational, but it sets a tone and expectation that everyone can understand and value because it underscores accountability.

ARE THE GOALS CLEAR? For each employee? Department? Team? If so, can you turn their schedule over to them to work out their own flexible work arrangement as long as they reach their goals? If they're not hitting their goals, are you certain that the goals are clear and the methods for achieving them are appropriate?

ALSO, YOU CAN NEGOTIATE flexibility and pay. If an employee wants more flexibility, he might have to take a reduction in pay. If they don't need as much flexibility, then he might be able to be paid more. It is a sliding scale – more of one means less of the other. Have your employees decide what they want; allow them to pick their own work arrangement and do your best to accommodate as long as the goals are routinely met.

FINALLY, SOME JOBS are not flexible. Are you being clear with those people that flexibility is not an option? Don't mislead them in any way.

CHAPTER SEVEN

THE MEANDERING CAREER PATH

Benefits of Nonlinear Advancement and Strong Career Advocates

IF A DEFINING CHARACTERISTIC of the young worker is a short attention span and eagerness to move on to the next interesting thing, it is logical that retaining them becomes more challenging. At the same time, this restlessness can present a great retention opportunity if viewed through the proper lens. Younger workers are typically eager for more – more information, more responsibility, more opportunity, more connections. Finding new ways to give them more, earlier in their careers, will strengthen their loyalty to you, and by extension, your organization.

Interestingly, the desire for a less linear career path is becoming more apparent across the generations as more individuals from all generations are looking at alternative careers. Whether it is because of corporate layoffs or the slow demise of entire industries, people are opening up their career plans to include complete shifts in industry and skill sets. Life-changing career moves are nothing new – *What Color is Your Parachute*, the quintessential guide to choosing the perfect career, was first released more than 15 years ago, when the economic boom gave people the courage to try new things. The difference is that today's economic turmoil is forcing people to reinvent themselves. *Whether by choice or by default, the end result is the same – the lifetime career is nearly extinct.* Malleable careers are the wave of the future.

NEW ROUTES TO LONG-TERM GROWTH

Back in the day, if you wanted to get from Chicago to L.A. there was one main path – Route 66. Similarly, in the corporate environment, the career path was predetermined – just climb the corporate ladder one rung at a time until you reach the top. Route 66 is now a vintage roadway, and the interstate highway system, not to mention air travel and video conferencing, offers endless ways to get from point A to point B (or to simply appear to be there). One may even skip point B and take a detour to Guatemala. The point? Choices. From an aisle full of cereals to 200+ television channels at the click of a button, the youngest generations *expect* options and want the opportunity to pursue different paths before making a commitment. Their careers are no different. Companies that successfully retain Millennial and Xer employees cater to this mobility trend by providing frequent evaluations, advancements, and opportunities for job change.

Not every career move within the organization is a linear advancement, however. Many companies promote the benefit of lateral moves – minimizing recruiting costs, maximizing each employee's experience and value to the organization, and tapping into the wanderlust of the younger generations. This is also a great retention tool when the numbers simply do not allow for direct ascension of the traditional hierarchy. Boomers are staying longer and therefore not making room for the usual promotions and advancement. These realities work together to create a new career path that meanders, navigating a spiral staircase or even a spider's web, rather than racing up a corporate ladder. Lateral moves combine with traditional advancements to keep younger generations engaged, challenged, and connected to your organization while searching for their rightful place within it.

In fact, Scott Klososky, who introduced us to the Ranks Off meeting, further advocates for diminishing hierarchy with his notion of the round organizational chart. In his plan, companies don't look at top-down management but rather focus on the customer view and delivering results. It's a radical change in perspective. What would your company look like if you drew a map from this vantage point? What career paths might open up?

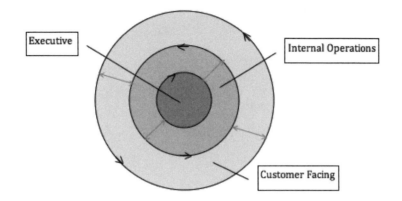

I've worked with Enterprise Rent-A-Car through the years and have been impressed by their approach to promotions. First, the company promotes from within at every opportunity. But even more to the point, promotions are fast and frequent. In a company recruiting video often shared at college career placement events, Enterprise employees are on camera discussing the multiple promotions they've held in a relatively short time frame. Recruits hear these snippets:

- *"I've been promoted nine times."*
- *"The first promotion I got when I was about three months into the company. It felt great."*
- *"I've had six promotions in nine years."*
- *"In a matter of a year, I got promoted three times."*
- *"Since working for the company, I've had four promotions. My friends are very jealous, they are still in the same spots they started in."*

Such rapid career changes are appealing to Millennials, who seek instant gratification, having grown up in a world that largely catered to their needs and made having it all seem eminently possible.

Before you start fearing budgets and knocking leaders off the ladder, it is important to point out that these frequent promotions do not have to look the same as traditional promotions. In fact, it is almost critical that they do not. The goal is to encourage and reward employees more quickly for their positive performance. You do not, however, want to promote an individual before they are ready.

As a result, frequent promotions are often mini promotions – a small salary increase, a slight title adjustment. *They are absolutely real, truthful recognitions of achievement; however they are more steppingstones between larger career advancements.* These steppingstones keep Millennials and Xers in the game long enough to make the more traditional advancements to leadership roles. They are also more flexible and customizable. A position does not have to come available for a promotion to happen, just a title change, etc., to recognize achievements for the company.

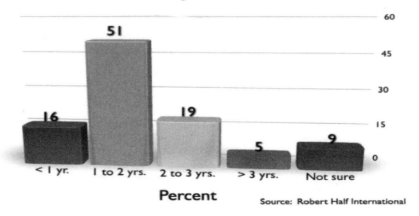

How long Millennials expect to have to "Pay their dues."

Source: Robert Half International

(Yahoo!hotjobs & Robert Half International[14])

Climbing a spiral staircase

The nontraditional career path at EF Education First is so ingrained in the company's culture that it actually has a name: the spiral staircase. EF employees are encouraged to seek out positions anywhere in the organization; in fact, the more diverse the better. It is all part of the company's belief in developing its employees and that there is no such thing as a lateral move.

Tessa Lorenze started her EF career in Cultural Care Au Pair as a regional manager for customer service. After 15 months, she was promoted to regional director. A year later, she moved to human resources as a recruitment manager for EF Center Boston, another division of the company. At the time of our interview, Lorenze was transitioning into a new role as the director of customer relations for EF Educational Tours, the company's largest educational travel division. Four years, four positions, three divisions, one company. Instead of looking at them as lost, EF views workers such as Lorenze as motivated students of the company. Such mobility and skill-broadening is integral to business success as well as personal growth. It also prevents boredom and burnout, and retains the company's investment in their training.

"We are a true people company, and we strongly believe in finding the right people and helping them grow professionally," said Martha Doyle, EF's chief administrative officer. "We continually challenge them and give them new responsibilities. *Along the way, they acquire new skills and new perspectives that help shape our business in creative and unexpected ways.* Plus, it keeps everybody engaged and motivated to learn new things, achieve new things and help move the company forward."

Variety is the spice of life
California-based Intuit is repeatedly listed as a desirable place to work by national surveys, including seven consecutive years on Fortune magazine's "100 Best Companies to Work For" list. The company offers flexibility to its employees through a Professional Development Rotation program that allows Intuit employees to move throughout the company, building skills and testing new areas of the employment. Similar to the traditional intern rotations in medical school, the Professional Development Rotation approach gives individuals the opportunity to experience a variety of career paths in hopes of finding the perfect fit.[15]

This is a more formal approach to building skills, with each employee spending a prescribed amount of time learning about each department. The goal is to have employees emerge with greater awareness of opportunities within the company and a stronger set of skills that can be applied anywhere within the organization.

This thinking ties in perfectly to the Millennial psyche of work, reward, and motivation; yet it also benefits Boomers and Xers who may be looking for different benefits, responsibilities, and interests at different stages of their careers. The common denominator in all these success stories is that each company makes it possible for employees to feel the benefit of hard work quickly by offering frequent rewards, while at the same time not tying employees to a defined career path. As a result, these companies can keep attrition rates low and focus their resources on growth rather than replacement.

One note while we discuss job descriptions, roles, and career paths overall: The structure of most large corporations provides both a defined framework for careers as well as a sheer volume of positions that can make room for flexibility. Small businesses, on the other hand, may be inherently more flexible in job descriptions but less able to restructure the hierarchy when there are significantly fewer positions available. A 10-person service company, for example, likely needs one or two administrative positions, one or two leadership roles, and six to eight client services staff. If the leaders are also the business owners, there is only so much room for advancement unless the company itself expands. In these situations, leaders can help keep employees on board longer by tweaking job descriptions to provide opportunities for individuals to expand their skills and practice different aspects of the business. With little room for advancement, they will naturally leave at some point; however, the period between joining and moving on can often be extended with creativity and conversation.

ROLE VS. DESCRIPTION

A key consideration when looking at adjustments to the traditional career structure is the distinction between a role and a job description. A job description is something you give to employees that tells them exactly what is expected of them each day. It outlines the processes and procedures clearly so there is no misunderstanding.

A person's *role* in the company is less specific. It is a macro versus a micro designation. *Role* refers to the value of a person's job. It includes how well an employee fits in and works with other departments, or how that person's work factors in with bottom-line priorities, such as sales and fulfillment. A person's role is the reason an employee works for the company, not the particular job. It is a motivator, not a task list. As such, employees can keep the same role while their job descriptions change with new responsibilities and minipromotions, preparing them for new roles further along.

The differences between a job description and a role are important:

- The job description is a step-by-step, play-by-play, description of how the job is to be executed.
- The role description offers less detail but gives an overall picture of the value of the job when executed properly.
- The job description details tasks.
- The role description defines responsibilities and why the job matters to the company and the customer.

In general, most employees who understand their role in the company will deliver. It's reassuring for them to understand how their work fits into the bigger picture. This is particularly true of the younger generations, who not only want to know their place but also want it spelled out for them. Managers may wish to see employees either work to understand their role or show the initiative to carve out a unique role, but the reality is that you will get the results you desire faster if *you* frame the role so they know where they fit in.

In their macro nature, roles also provide some room for expression and fluidity, where perhaps a job description is more confining. A role empowers someone to figure out a better way, while the job description places boundaries on the day. Taking the time to identify the role each person plays in the company is therefore critical to setting the stage for engaged, committed employees who want to do more for your organization. And as a result, they can advance in a variety of ways, keeping strong talent within the company, whether the individual follows a traditional or meandering career path. It may be well worth your time to become versed in your employees' roles so that you can discuss them with regularity and ease. Remember, roles are motivational.

TAKEAWAYS

The traditional corporate ladder is mostly gone. To meet the expectations of today's employee and to keep them around long enough to add sustained value to your organization, it is crucial to rethink policies and habits surrounding roles, responsibilities, promotions, and career paths.

- Consider smaller, but more frequent career changes – minipromotions and/or adding responsibilities to an existing role.
- Look throughout the organization, not just up and down the chain of command, to find the right fit for quality talent. Perhaps you have a great details person in marketing who should be in accounting. If the work ethic and personality fit the corporate culture, try hard to find the right job for that individual.
- Embrace lateral moves as part of company culture – it speaks to the generational desire for constantly doing new things, while allowing time to gain more skills before more traditional advancements. Lateral moves also help find a person's true role in the company.
- Value well-rounded skills, making opportunities available for individuals to learn about roles outside their department, perhaps even trying on different jobs before settling in.
- Take the time to define the role of each individual, in addition to their actual job description. It may, in turn, help define their unique career path.
- Discuss the role with each employee in person. A more organic, interpersonal distinction than the job description, the role is a conversation, not a to-do list.
- Be creative with career advancements. If valued employees do not covet the jobs traditionally ahead of them, work to determine how they can continue to grow their careers through lateral moves or changes in job responsibilities. Keep it interesting to keep them engaged. Get their input as to what role they want in the company.
- Create individual plans for career growth. Do not rely on the same model that has been applied to every employee for 30 years. This generation wants custom solutions and will go where their distinct qualities are recognized.

MOVE OVER MENTORS, HELLO ADVOCATES.

IN THE COURSE OF A meandering career path, mentors and advocates are increasingly important. Movement simply for the sake of motion is not always ideal. Millennials, who have largely had their parents or peers helping shape their decision-making to date, are eager for wise counsel and will seek out individuals they admire and trust to help make sense of their career goals.

The best such relationships occur naturally between employee and advocate, and are supported by the organization through available time, lunch-n-learns and other opportunities to connect up and down the organizational structure.

What is the difference between a mentor and an advocate? The role of the mentor is typically someone who draws their expertise and advice from looking backwards upon their own career and presenting that historical viewpoint to the next in line. They are passing down skills in anticipation of being replaced, and there are times and places where this is extremely valuable. Advocates, however, look to the future from the perspective of the person they champion. They focus on where a person can go, what they can do, what they can become; then they help outline how to get there. Because the focus is on the person, not the job, an advocate does not even need to be in the same field or line of business as the person she advocates for – the relationship and general business experience is more important than a specific skill set.

Mentor: Do this.
Advocates: How can we help you?

Mentor: This is what you get.
Advocate: What do you need from us to do your job better?

Mentor: You're not quite ready for that job yet, just be patient. You need to prove yourself here for a while first.
Advocate: What can we do for you to get you where you want to go?

Generational preferences have shaped the move from mentorship to advocacy, and, frankly, many organizations out there have mentor programs that have fallen flat and are only discussed in hushed voices, if at all. They're a taboo subject because a lot of time was put into the mentor program with negligible results. Advocacy is a more grass-roots approach, and as such, is often more appealing to leaders, employees and organizations as a whole.

One of the reasons that mentor relationships have failed so many times is that the Boomers are proving to be poor mentors. It isn't that they don't have insights to share; it's that they're incredibly busy, and the Boomers will be the first ones to agree. Many of them are working harder at this point in their career than when they joined the workforce. And today's Great Recession is spurring a need to work to do even more with less and to try not to be one of the ones cut if the company has to trim jobs. The Boomers have the added pressures of children who are remaining reliant upon them much later in life and now the Boomers' parents are making noises about moving in with their children because of their deteriorating health. They watched their workplace predecessors begin to slightly scale back at this same point in their careers but the Boomers are experiencing nothing like that. They're still go-go-go, and the thought of taking on a mentee is not something they're excited to do. They know they should help, but their time is already full. For this reason they may be much more inclined to begin an advocate relationship over a mentor relationship. An advocate relationship requires less of a commitment but still helps move someone toward individual goals. Easier and quicker – nothing wrong with that. Especially to a busy Boomer.

Strong advocate relationships help employees feel connected to the organization and more compelled to seek opportunity from within rather than believing they must move elsewhere to gain new skills and experiences. This can result in more satisfaction from the employee and greater retention for the business, with the added benefit of bringing fresh energy and enthusiasm to different positions without the training and assimilation expense of completely new hires.

A MATCH MADE IN HUMAN RESOURCES?

IF THE YOUNGER GENERATIONS are apprehensive of forced relationships and distrustful of unproven leaders, how does an organization promote advocate relationships? There are several ways to do this, ranging from the informal to the carefully structured. All, however, leave room for chemistry, the unpredictable element that indicates an ability to work well together despite surface differences.

Many companies I've worked with find that the first step is making strong internal networks a stated corporate value. From the boardroom to the mailroom, interdepartmental networks are encouraged and even required. At more than one company, an employee's network is actually part of the formal review process. Employees must reveal their connections and relationships throughout the organization, demonstrating where they worked together across departments and how they understand the role their position plays in the greater picture of the organization. These networks may not yield specific advocate relationships, but they do encourage sharing of information and increase an employee's ability to know about and take advantage of career opportunities outside of their current business line or subject area.

EF Education First recently overhauled its formal mentor program, replacing traditional assigned mentor relationships with informal, open networking opportunities. The company now offers regular Career Chats, where members of the leadership team hold round-table discussions with interested employees. These events are open to all employees but not required of any. As a result, employees who attend are actively interested and engaged in the conversation, ensuring a productive meeting that is a valuable use of everyone's time. Attendees learn more about what is going on in different areas of the company, possibly piquing interest for future job changes, and career leaders have the opportunity to connect with the future of the company to share their ideas and advice.

A side benefit of the Career Chats is that employees and leaders who may never have met through the course of a regular workweek are introduced and natural advocate opportunities arise.

"It's amazing how many new professional connections emerge from our Career Chats," EF's Martha Doyle said. "Those chats lead to new ideas, new opportunities and even new friendships. It gives employees in our student travel divisions, for example, a chance to learn about our exchange programs. Those connections help all of us — from entry-level staff to regional managers to division presidents —to widen our professional networks and develop other relationships to rely on for information and advice."

While organic advocate relationships tend to yield strong results, formal programs also have their place in today's business environment. Deloitte, which has also been a frequent flier on the Fortune Best Companies list, recently introduced its Future Leaders Apprentice Program (FLAP) to support recruiting efforts among experienced minorities and high-potential college students. While arguably launched for recruiting purposes, FLAP includes a strong advocacy component.[16]

The company identifies potential leaders through its recruiting efforts. Recruits are offered a scholarship toward undergraduate expenses or pursuit of the CPA designation and, in return, they agree to work for Deloitte upon graduation. At Deloitte, FLAP recruits are enrolled in a two-year leadership development curriculum that includes multiple networking opportunities, introducing these high-potential young employees to all areas of the organization. To further promote those critical advocate relationships, Deloitte matches each FLAP participant with mid- and/or senior-level managers who guide them through career decisions.

TAKEAWAYS

Creating strong relationships within the organization provides a benefit to both the employee and the company. Many Millennials were somewhat coddled through their early years, at least by "old school" standards, and are accustomed to having someone looking out for their best interests. An advocate serves that role, connecting the individual to the company without taking away the element of choice. To support this function in your organization:

- Demonstrate value for the advocate role by offering training and/ or time during the normal workday to dedicate to the advisee.
- Coach advocates to focus on the goals of the advisee, not the company. Eventually, they will meet.
- Ask more questions – advocates should be interested in the person, learning how they can help, not lecturing on the right way to accomplish traditional goals.
- Look outside the department or division for potential advocate matches to minimize issues and assumptions related to traditional boss/employee hierarchies
- Be flexible – don't be afraid to make changes if personalities do not connect. It is all about the relationship and open communication, not specific skills to be passed on.

TO THINK ON...

• **CONSIDER THE CAREER** track in your company and ask yourself why it is this way. Is it something you inherited in your position and, thus, has always been this way? Is it something you cobbled together as you grew your company or your department and there is no real reason ... it just *is*. Or is there a strategy for the way your career path functions? If there is a strategy, is that strategy still valid considering today's workforce and today's economy? Are there changes that you can make to adjust to today's changed workforce that will accommodate your needs and those of your staff? What are those changes and how can you begin to implement them?

• **SIMPLE AND INSTANT** pieces of recognition are important for both new employees and young employees. Can you create some titles or something similar to recognize levels of achievement in the job that aren't exactly promotions but do recognize substantive advancement in the job?

• **MANY DEPARTMENTS OF** large companies tend to treat teammates who have moved into a different division of the company like mutineers, like these people have offended their former teammates. Considering the career demands of today's employees, having people move from department to department is a much better option than losing them. Is there resentment when a teammate moves from one place to another? Or encouragement that they're broadening their scope of the company? How can you change the attitude within your organization to support those who transfer within the organization?

• **DO YOUR EMPLOYEES** know their role? Have you ever discussed it with them? It's likely that they know their job description, but what about their role? Often managers reply with "they should just know," but that is a poor answer – your time in your company has given you an understanding of a role. People newer to the organization don't have the benefit of time to distinguish their role vs. their job description, regardless of their generation. Have you ever articulated the role? Written it down? It clears up a lot of confusion when an employee can read it for himself and know how his job supports the role.

CHAPTER EIGHT

BETWEEN THE OFFER AND THE EXIT

Get Recruits Connected and Engaged from Day One

If the younger generations are looking to advocates more for career advice than for building skills and they desire speedy advancement, then training and development become increasingly important. Remember, this is a generation tuned in to rapid advancement, increasing education demands and a strong preference for "edutainment." They are lifelong learners at the tender age of 20-something, having been introduced to flashcards shortly after birth. Yes, I'm exaggerating. But not by much. Many members of the Xer and Millennial generations are simply accustomed to constant education. This is good news for training departments in many ways — here is a new crop of employees with a touch of youthful omnipotence, but also a genuine desire to know even more. The downside, of course, is figuring out how to deliver that knowledge in a way that keeps them interested and engaged. In addition, you need to consider how to meet the training needs at all levels among very disparate learning preferences.

At Enterprise, the guidance begins before the first day of work. New recruits are often matched up with a First Day Buddy who shares the inside scoop on where to park, what to bring, etc. This simple gesture demonstrates to new employees that they are part of a community that wants them to succeed. It also helps alleviate first-day jitters by providing a peer resource for asking the questions that often make new employees feel foolish. The real corporate level training is still provided, of course, but the introduction and workplace insight is a nice added touch.

EATING THE ELEPHANT

Early on in his management career, David Houchins recognized a distinct difference in the way his Boomer and Millennial staff sought training. Boomers still wanted a full syllabus outlining everything they would learn and when they would learn it. Much like the corporate ladders they are climbing, Boomers need to see the path. And on paper, if you don't mind. Xers would like to see the details – just to be sure you've really thought everything through – but they only want to spend time discussing the big picture. Millennials, on the other hand, just want to know that the information is there when they need it.

"When I talk about our agency's and my team's training program with Boomers they want to know the details and they want to hold it in their hands and see how the entire process is laid out, class by class, hour by hour," Houchins states. "But if I start down that path with my young recruits, handing over paper and outlining three years of scheduled training, their eyes glaze over. They don't want to receive that level of detail all at once. I had to find a new way to discuss the process in order to keep their interest. Now we don't talk about learning tracts, we talk about eating an elephant."

Yes, Houchins' Millennial recruits now discover training as a pachyderm buffet. He recognized that the Boomers want to see the program in its entirety while the Xers want to know what the plan is and that it is going to work. Millennials, however, don't want the plan; they just want to know that the company has everything under control. If we were to eavesdrop on the conversation it would go something like this:

Houchins: Our training program is kind of like an elephant. Have you ever eaten an elephant?

Millennial: Uh, no.

Houchins: Have you ever contemplated eating an elephant?

Millennial: Don't be ridiculous.

Houchins: Well, if you were to eat an elephant where would you start?

Millennial: (Blank stare, possibly a reflexive eye roll)

Houchins: Well, if you were to eat an elephant, you'd need to start dividing it up. Our training is like that — it's a beast, with lots you need to consume. There are at least three years' worth of lessons and courses to get you where you ultimately want to go in our sales force. That could be over-whelming if you let it.

Millennial: Sounds like it.

Houchins: Well, I've quartered the elephant for you to make it easier to digest. There are four broad subject areas, each containing dozens of topics and learning opportunities. Those details aren't important right now. But what you need to know is that it is all in there and available to you. We've got a recommended approach, but there's some flexibility to make sure that you get everything you need at the right time. Sound good?

Millennial: Sure.

Houchins: So ultimately it's my job to help you devour the whole ele-phant. I'll put on your plate only what you need and can digest at the moment. We'll get you through it and if you have any questions or are inter-ested in any of the details at any time, I have the whole process outlined back at my office, so just ask.

For the Millennial, knowing that the information is available and has been thought through by the leadership is enough. When he's ready for the next bite, he'll ask. Better yet, Houchins can demonstrate five-star service and present the next course at just the right time.

SHOW THEM THE BLACKBERRY

Perks indicate importance. That's really the bottom line. And while perks have a price tag, they need not be incredibly pricey. Furthermore, the cost of the perk is often quickly outweighed by the value of loyalty — engaged, productive employees contribute more to the bottom line and reduce the hard and soft costs associated with employee turnover.

Millennials, especially, view technology perks as must-haves in a profes-sional environment. Yes, they already have cell phones and internet connections, but many are branching off on their own for the first time, so moving those expenses from the parental payroll to the company dime represents a significant value. Beyond economic impact, however, the company-issue Blackberry offers a secondary message "you are important – we need to be able to reach you." And thirdly, offering mobile technology further supports the Millennial tendency toward nontraditional work hours. Simple perk, deep-running results.

What about companies facing hard economic times? Shouldn't perks be the first to go? Not always. If the choice is to stop paying employee cell phone bills or to lay off staff, then yes, the cell phones may need to go on hiatus. However I caution businesses to closely evaluate the positive effects perks have on employees before erroneously slashing budgets.

Internet giant Google has long been known for its innovative, entrepreneurial spirit with workplace perks ranging from daily catered lunches to on-site game rooms and bring-your-dog-to-work day (which, actually, is everyday). In 2008 the company's stock fell 26 percent along with most of the NASDAQ. Yet, according to officials interviewed for a Charlotte Observer news article, management did not slash every perk in an effort to control costs. ... They nipped and tucked, removing first those perks that were less frequently used (afternoon tea at the New York office, a video production studio at the Mountain View, California, location). Officials cited that upfront costs of buying games and decor and the recurring food and drink expenses are small compared to the long-term payoff of these signature Google perks.[17]

I will say it again: Happy employees are good employees. Dollars spent on making employees feel valued have direct bottom-line results. In fact, if you are in a position where deep cuts need to be made and perks are on the line, I encourage you to engage employees in the discussion. You may be surprised at which benefits they are willing to give up and the ways they can find to reduce costs in order to keep certain perks.

TAKEAWAYS

All employees want to feel valued. With the younger generations, that value is demonstrated by investing in them through perks and training. The key is to match the perks and training styles with the types of workers you have on staff.

- Engage Millennials with interactive training, both online and interpersonal – it needs to be entertaining to stick with them. Provide flexibility in the sequence where possible.
- Boomers tend to be more studious in nature, seeking access to the whole program and tackling it systematically.
- Look at the perks your management and higher-ups are receiving – paid internet, telecom packages or parking access, for example, and determine where that may be appropriate for lower level employees.
- Consider incremental perks based on time on the job, creating incentives for staying with the company longer. Remember, after three years the likelihood of staying with a company increases exponentially.

TRAINING AS A STATUS SYMBOL

An international prestige cosmetics company has hit on a training program that provides different experiences for different levels of employees, taps into the generational desire to be both part of a team and able to contribute at a higher level, and prepares employees for advancing through the company to leadership roles. This internal leadership training is divided into three distinct programs, each of which requires college admissions-style entry with letters of recommendation and personal essays to demonstrate one's ability, commitment to the organization, and readiness for the intense program.

You, Inc. is a yearlong training program for entry-level employees. Candidates for the program must be top performers, have at least one year of tenure in the position and submit two letters of recommendation as well as an essay about why they want to participate. Initiative and effectiveness are critical components for determining who enters each class. Through *You, Inc.* these employees, who are mostly young and new to the company, are exposed to high-level leaders, learn negotiating techniques, and work on a specific project or case which they present to company leadership at the close of the program. The goal of this training level is to teach employees to think of themselves as a brand, that they are in charge of their own brand equity and that they must market themselves in the workplace.

You, Inc. is a creative solution to the common complaint of younger generations not demonstrating enough ownership over their careers. Instead of lamenting the problem, this company embraced it with training designed to encourage self-awareness and promotion.

The next phase of the program, *Bring Out Your Best*, takes aim at the assistant manager and manager levels, while *Strategic Think* works with directors and executives. Again, all participants are self-selected – they must choose to embark on this journey and meet the requirements in order to become part of the annual class. Both *Bring Out Your Best* and *Strategic Think* move from the business and career savvy focus of *You, Inc.* to strategic problem solving with a corporate perspective. The participants are given high-level, real-world business cases to solve and work in multifunctional teams to generate creative results.

These business cases are far beyond the normal scope of the participants' regular job descriptions, reinforcing the notion that good ideas have power no matter where they come from, as we discussed with Scott Klososky. In fact, the manager I spoke with confirmed that the solutions generated by *Bring Out Your Best* and *Strategic Think* teams in the past have saved the company almost $10 million combined.

To illustrate the value of the solutions formed in this intensive training program, my contact gave the example of a recent case that involved improving utilization of marketing collateral at the regional and store levels. Some costly materials were simply sitting in storage at some retail sites while other locations were going through supplies faster than expected. The financial impact was enough to warrant hiring a well-known, high-end consultant for recommendations. Meanwhile, the sitting *Bring Out Your Best* class was also working on the problem as a test case. In the end, the company reviewed both recommendations and chose the solution developed by the training team, who, incidentally, cost them nothing extra.

This underscores the value of such dedicated initiatives – the company saves money and increases loyalty while the employee receives robust, career-enhancing experience and gains an incredible internal network. "These programs take a look at our top talent and give them a real development plan," said a human resources manager at the company. "We demonstrate loyalty to the employee, provide them with an incredibly valuable and practical business education, and they deliver results. It is also a great jump start to a promotion as the program is a true proving ground for talent." It's no wonder individuals are clamoring for a space in the program each year.

TAKEAWAYS

Proper training is imperative. It not only prepares an employee to do his best work in his current position, but it can also provide growth opportunities within the company. Look at training for specific skills required by specific jobs, but also at the softer skills of good leaders. If younger employees don't have career development knowledge coming in, consider offering it to them in the form of company training.

- Look at career development as an opportunity and a responsibility – you can watch your future leaders handle management situations and be prepared with the right training so they are ready when the time comes.
- Remember that you cannot hold people accountable for things they do not know. Company-sponsored business training allows you to provide that general knowledge with a company-specific slant.
- Career development is a networking opportunity as well as a training ground.
- Make it real – give them actual, current business problems to solve. If you implement their ideas, give them credit.
- Positioned and implemented properly, training is viewed as a valuable incentive, not a burden.

═══ TO THINK ON... ═══

• YOU MAY SEE LITTLE perks as frivolous things that cloud the real reason people should want to work for you. But to some employees they really matter, and for that reason they should matter to you. What can you do for them to signify that they're important to you?

• ARE THERE CHALLENGES within your organization that you can utilize to train your staff? Issues you need addressed where you can assemble a team of employees from all departments to solve and, in the process, help them learn the company, the market, and/or the opportunities this issue provides? Is there a way for them to compete for these positions? What about a way to make these positions cherished and highly visible?

• WHAT DOES A NEW employee see at your company or in your department on Day 1? Remember, you never get a second chance to make a first impression. How can you make sure Day 1 is a total success and gives your new employee the right impression about you and your team? Can you script it out? That Day 1 experience likely makes such a big impression that it will be hard to alter opinions down the road.

• TRAINING IS A RETENTION tool, especially for the younger team members. Are you offering enough training? It is easy to look at it only as an expense with a hard-to-define return on investment. If there were an opportunity to invest in a program called Employee Retention Assurance, would you? Might that actually be what training is?

CHAPTER NINE

JOIN THE HERD

Creating and Managing an Increasingly Social Workplace Environment

A DISTINCT CHARACTERISTIC of the Millennial generation is their strong herd mentality – they do things together, whether it be housing, extracurricular activity, or even job interviews. Being connected to one another is not just a desire, but an integral part of their cultural DNA. As a result, the best workplace environment – the one most likely to attract, engage, and retain Millennials – is one where there are opportunities to work in teams and to socialize with peers. Company-supported social activities facilitate the ability to connect with one another and increase positive associations with the workplace.

Millennials are also connected with the world at large. A sense of altruism runs through this generation, and their optimistic personalities make them well-suited for community outreach. Allowing employee-generated volunteer experiences to take place within the work environment – either through paid volunteer time off or organized groupwide volunteer efforts – allows them to honor that piece of themselves, while connecting the company and the community it serves. Incidentally, Matures and Boomers can be great advocates for this type of venture now that many are finding themselves with empty homes and more time to devote to volunteer efforts. This presents another opportunity for younger generations to network throughout all areas and levels of the organization, increasing their overall engagement and exposure.

CLUB MILLENNIAL

MILLENNIALS HAVE A seemingly ingrained need to be part of something larger than themselves. This manifests in both their herd like social structures and their altruistic attitudes. And yet this is still the same generation that grew up with parents more focused on their children's self-esteem than perhaps any other time in history. *The need to be considered special still holds true. So how does that manifest in professional environments?*

With little acknowledgement of the separation of work and personal life thanks to the 24/7 nature of the world they grew up in, Millennials tend to look toward their working peers for some level of social camaraderie. More so than generations before them, Millennials want to truly befriend their coworkers. What starts with the occasional drink after hours often morphs into genuine friendships that last beyond the employment terms. This can present a conundrum for peers as they advance to management and also for managers seeking to stay connected to the individual while maintaining an appropriate degree of professionalism, as we have already discussed.

But understanding that younger employees often seek more out of their workplace relationships presents leaders with an opportunity to deliver more value to their Millennial workers while increasing their satisfaction with and affinity for the workplace.

IF YOU BUILD IT, THEY WILL COME

PERHAPS ONE OF the most comprehensive examples of social structures being created by an organization for the benefit of its youngest employees is the GRAD program at Harris Corporation. In an effort to attract qualified recruits to its corporate campus in Melbourne, Florida – a community more known for its retirement benefits than its youthful social scene – Harris Corp took matters into its own hands.

The GRAD (GRaduate Acclimation Development) Program offers the company's newest recruits a quick and easy way to connect with their peers and learn more about both Harris and the surrounding community. Membership in GRAD is paid for by the company for the first year. After that employees pay annual dues for access to the activities and programs, ensuring that it is a value-laded program offering a variety of social and volunteer opportunities that appeal to both single recruits and young families.

EMBRACING A TRADITION OF COMMUNITY

A FAST-PACED SOCIAL SCENE is also part of the company culture at EF Education First. Based in Boston, with numerous colleges nearby to fuel recruiting, EF doesn't need to woo its employees to the city. But it does need to make them want to stay on board once they get there. A 45-year-old company with a largely Xer and Millennial staff, EF has figured out how to remain fresh, relevant and professional.

One of the company's core values is to retain the entrepreneurial spirit that has fueled a half-century of success. Some traditions remain and others have evolved over time. At EF, holidays are a time of great celebration within the company, offering opportunities to come together at the office, on company time, to enjoy each other's companionship.

The holiday social scene includes two company-driven traditions and one employee-sparked event. To put its own spin on the standard office holiday party, EF hosts an annual holiday open house for friends and family. EF opens the doors and allows employees to share their workplace with those who are important in their lives. While not created for this purpose alone, the friends-and-family aspect of this event ties in extremely well to the Millennial yearning for validation from peers and parents.

Each year during the open house, EF honors its Swedish roots by celebrating Santa Lucia Day, a traditional Scandinavian holiday. The celebration includes staffers and company au pairs performing a candlelit Santa Lucia procession, while all join in to sing a traditional Swedish song. Although the Santa Lucia is not a typical social event, it represents a strong sense of tradition and being connected to something larger than oneself – a perfect match for the Millennial psyche.

Stepping away from the serious and engaging the silly, EF also supports an annual employee-run Halloween costume contest, in which entire departments will often coordinate themes and compete for bragging rights. Years past have included the Queens of HR (with costumes ranging from the Queen of Hearts to the Queen of the Nile) and the Finance Superheroes. This inexpensive event is a social rallying point that encourages EF staffers to have fun and strengthen bonds among teams and throughout the organization.

SOCIAL SUCCESS OR TOTAL PARTY FOUL

WHAT'S THAT? You've tried team-building events and they just don't work? Everyone grumbles about spending a Saturday on the ropes course or being made to perform silly skits? The Xers don't want to be away from their kids, the Boomers are too established to bother and the Millennials are just annoyed? Of course.

There are three notable differences between social efforts that work and those that fall flat. First and foremost, team building is not the explicit intent. Second, successful efforts are largely optional. And finally, they are best driven by the employees themselves. If the company sends out the decree to "please begin having fun now," the initiative is simply doomed. Getting employees on board and letting them shape the event is critical for success.

Take the Halloween costume contest at EF, for example. The No. 1 purpose of the event? Have fun. Business line teams coming together with thematic costumes is a natural offshoot, not a corporate edict. And while peer pressure likely plays a part in some employees' decisions to participate or not, there is no top-down edict that requires anyone to forego their suit and tie for a superhero cape and tights. In fact, perhaps that one should be actively discouraged. The decision to participate is left up to each individual. The desire to participate, however, is greatly increased by the sheer fact the employees get together to plan the event – creating a grassroots enthusiasm for the afternoon of absurdity. The announcement of a companywide costume party is therefore met with excitement rather than a collective eye roll. And no one fears for his or her job if they politely decline to join in.

At Clarity, the team has tapped into a reality-TV phenomenon to create fun social opportunities. A bimonthly potluck meal has morphed into an Iron Chef theme, tapping into a both a shared interest in cooking and the competitive spirit of a sales-driven organization. The opportunity for creating casual, interactive social outlets is pretty far-reaching. It just takes some time planning and figuring out what clicks for your staff.

WHEN IS IT OKAY TO BE THE HOST?

SO FAR, MOST OF these socializing best practices are company-sponsored, employee-driven. You may be asking when it's acceptable for the company to take the reins and control the event. That opportunity comes with strategic planning retreats and social rewards. These are excellent opportunities to orchestrate mandatory social activities that are aligned with stated business goals.

Timothy Conley, a managing director at an international environmental consulting firm, recently restructured a company social perk to create a more direct connection with sales and customer relations. The result far exceeded expectations:

"Our team had a standing practice of attending Oktoberfest as an expenses-paid team-building event. We would invite all of our European employees, covering travel, room and board," Conley explains. "After a few years, staff began to take it for granted and sometimes not even show up, resulting in cancellation fees and missed networking opportunities. They simply did not realize the value of the event."

"This year, I changed the invitation rules," Conley continues. "Staff must now pay their own travel and rooms if they want to attend … unless they are successful in getting a client or potential client to the event. We will have more clients then ever at the event this year."

This is an excellent example of a company recognizing that the social reward has lost its purpose and needs to be more closely tied to business goals. It also underscores what I've witnessed around the world – employees want to perform well; they just need the encouragement to do so. *Millennials will rise to the challenge and earn their social opportunities because they do value the ability to relax and connect with their peers.*

TAKEAWAYS

Avoid common pitfalls when creating social opportunities for your team.

- Seek input from employees to determine what is interesting to them.
- Offer a variety of options, allowing employees to pick and choose where they join in.
- Do not promote a social event and then sneak training in. Make the professional-social connection clear.
- Tie big social rewards to professional goals, such as mini getaways for meeting team goals, to reinforce the importance of productivity, not just having fun.

CAPTURING AND CONNECTING THE NEXT GENERATION

THE STATISTICS SURROUNDING the financial planning industry are grim — a very discernible graying of the profession is occurring. The median age of financial planners is 52 years old. At a 2004 Advanced Planners Retreat held by the industry's largest professional association, only four or five of the 250-300 attendees were younger than 30. About 80 percent to 90 percent were 50 or older. Looking at that disparity and the upcoming lack of qualified professionals filling the pipeline, it is easy to see why recruiting, retention, and knowledge transfer are huge buzzwords in the field today. What may be different here is that these younger financial planners have looked around, realized they are relatively peerless, and are trying to do something about it, from the bottom up.

Following that lopsided retreat, Michael Kitces, the financial adviser we met in Chapter Six, joined forces with Aaron Coates of Relevant Financial Planning and some other fellow Millennial/Xer planners to form an online group for young financial planners (the group defines "young" as under 36; I'll let you decide how you feel about that number). Using word of mouth only, they rounded up 20-30 fellow young planners to launch NexGen. The simple, bare-bones group functions as a virtual community, with an online Yahoo! group as its only location. Since its launch, NexGen has almost doubled in size each year, and now boasts 300-400 members. With the growing interest in NexGen, the original leaders recently decided to organize a real world meet-up and scheduled a two-and-a-half-day conference in Colorado. More than half of the membership attended this inaugural event.

"The thing that stands out to me about NexGen is the way members come to us," Kitces said. "I get e-mails and calls all the time from people who say 'I heard there is a group out there for people like me, I just want to be part of it.' They don't even know what it is, but they want to join. The nature of the financial planner employee experience in particular can be very isolating and these young professionals are just aching to find a community."

Kitces further notes that professional associations in the industry have tried to formally replicate NexGen for other special interest groups with far less success. The generational gap is the only answer he's found – Millennials are simply much more comfortable operating in a virtual world, and their peer-to-peer bond has far more impact than one based solely on a specialized topic of interest. They view their NexGen peers with as much respect and camaraderie as they do the associate sitting across the office, if not more so.

JUMP IN, GET AHEAD

THE NEED FOR COMMUNITY is absolute among all people, but the reliance on peer testimony and social networks is exceedingly obvious among the younger generations. After all, these are the creators of epinions.com, where we can find peer reviews of nearly any product, and MySpace/Facebook/Twitter, where we can stay connected with anyone and everyone despite logistics. Proactively creating a space for this type of community can make a huge impact on the speed with which individuals make the connection.

Institutions as steadfast and traditional as the U.S. Navy have taken notice, as I learned on a once-in-a-lifetime visit to spend 24 hours aboard the USS Harry Truman, the Navy's newest aircraft carrier at the time. They were conducting carrier qualifications for the pilots off the coast of North Carolina. A military influence is one of the indicators for individuals who may not fit their generational stereotype, so I was curious as to why the Navy would feel the need to bring me in to discuss generational discord. When I got aboard I learned that the average age on deck, outside the pilots, is 19 years old. So while most corporations have only a few Millennials in place, this environment was teeming with them, making it a great proving ground for new approaches to motivating this group.

One of the things the Navy offers to all sailors, but mainly used by the Millennials is an on-ship profile page, similar to a MySpace page. The Navy realized that their recruits were used to using MySpace but that it was a security risk to allow that level of social networking to be broadcast to friends to and from the ship. To meet the need, the Navy created something similar for their sailors. The ship's system serves the same purpose but is used to connect the shipmates – there can be thousands of them – as well as to provide an outlet for demonstrating one's individual personality and helping shipmates learn more about one another. Despite being confined to a single aircraft carrier, these Millennial sailors are using technology to reach out to one another. It is just one more example of how truly different each generation is, and how important it is that organizations adjust to the fundamental needs of each.

Even the state of Oklahoma has tapped into this need for peer networks and is using the online world to facilitate it. Project Boomerang, an initiative of the Oklahoma Department of Commerce, is aimed at reaching out to "elsewhere Oklahomans" and convincing them to return home, where jobs are available and the lifestyle is both family-friendly and increasingly hip. The project centers on a website, www.okboomerang.com, where current residents share their own boomerang stories – why they left, why they came back, and why the love it.[18] Sure, the site contains practical DOC information – housing information, video tours of main cities and rural areas alike, facts and figures, affordability calculators, and job listings from Boomerang partners – but the hook is the interactive testimonials. Not only are there select "boomerang Oklahoman" stories on the home page, but the testimonials page functions as a blog of sorts, allowing members to share their own stories of returning home. Prospective workers get the "been there, done that" stories from their peers – individuals who likely have similar interests and reservations and who are willing to share, unedited, why they love the decision they made.

TAKEAWAYS

Creating a community within your workforce is different today than it was 30 years ago. It is more than just team meetings and common workplace goals; there is a social component that was not part of the picture before. But it is important to creating a connected workplace.

- Tap into the desire to share opinions – ask your employees to help build your social infrastructure, or just validate what they are already creating.
- Use the Internet. Today's worker is accustomed to sharing information online and places a high value on peer feedback, whether or not they've met.
- Consider intranet forums for specific topics – perhaps around social/diversity issues or job functions. Give individuals a place to connect and discuss informally.
- Create Twitter sites and Facebook pages for your company and allow the Millennials to take charge in keeping these sites current, bearing in mind that these are customer-focused sites, not internal chat rooms, which should dictate the content that is placed on them.
- Encourage occasional, more formalized get-togethers to increase the connection.

IF YOU LEAD, WILL THEY FOLLOW?

IF YOU'VE GOT social opportunities in place – either from years of tradition or new ideas brought forth from the ranks – you may find that Xer managers are less than thrilled about getting involved. How can you get them on board? As a whole, Xers tend to disdain team-building events and company picnics, seeing them as fake or forced socializing. Whereas Boomers live at work and Millennials see work as one more social outlet, Xers draw clear distinctions between work and play. *They are more than capable of leading their teams from a business standpoint, but their cynical, loner attitudes are deeply embedded, even while serving in leadership positions.* And they still have strong opinions on the sanctity of personal time. They simply don't show up at the Christmas party at the boss's house, and this causes problems within the organization. So, again the question, how do get them to participate?

The answer goes back to what we discussed in Chapter 5 – an employee's cost vs. value. When an employee in a leadership position does not participate in the important company functions and when her absence is notable because of her position, she significantly decreases her value. This is a conversation that needs to be had with this employee. Better still, have a conversation prior to promoting this type of Xer to a new position of leadership. If she hasn't been gung ho about company events to date, don't expect that to change just because she's in management. Make no assumptions about what you think should be common knowledge. A direct conversation is required in which it is made clear that participation in certain events is expected of managers and that lack of participation is harmful to the company, to the job, and to her career.

But before we rake Xers over the coals, it is also worth considering the true value of these events over time. Many of them – ropes course team building and some retreats, for example – sit squarely on the values of the Boomer generation, including consensus building, face time and company championship. Sometimes Xers are right in believing them to be "Kumbaya" events that lack a real purpose other than perceived community building. So it is important to ask, "Why are we doing this? What do we expect to get out of it? What is the motivation for people to attend other than we'd like them to? Are they fun? Educational? Beneficial in any way other than to those of us who think they are?"

Consider pulling your employees together and asking how the company can develop a sense of community within itself other than through a company picnic, which may be attended by your younger team members with reservations and a chip on their shoulders for giving you time that isn't compensated for on their paychecks. Explain your goals, what you want the outcome to be. How do you define a sense of community within the company, what does it look and feel like, and is there another way to achieve it? And let them take it over for a try.

Remember, the boss who says "Please begin having fun/liking each other

... Now!" understands the need for connection but doesn't see how to help it along. He's following the letter of the law, while ignoring the spirit behind it. *Connectivity is an organic, living thing. The company must support it, offering room and time for it to grow, but it cannot demand it.* Try turning community building over to your team members – give them the desired outcome and then allow them to pick the path.

TAKEAWAYS

Hold on to the Boomer need for community building, but let go of the picture in your mind. Community looks different today – it can be virtual or centered around giving. It can include family or never cross that line. Xers and Millennials have different approaches to similar goals, and as the Boomers have largely secured their connections, it is time to let the younger generations have a turn.

- Look at what your company offers and what it demands. Is it working?
- Make sure new managers, especially younger ones, know exactly what is expected from them on the social front – preferably before they take the position.
- Be prepared to dial back the number of required events, or to change the way they look to meet today's needs and interests.
- Always be strategic and relevant, not just habitual. Time-honored traditions still have their place, just use them appropriately. Sometimes the value is simply in telling the company story, and that can be just as important as face time and networking.

TO THINK ON...

• **FOR THE YOUNGEST** employees, company loyalty and peer loyalty often go together. Work to create an environment in which the employees are active together outside the workplace. If they want to create a softball team, encourage it and allow space internally to display game schedules or results. Create opportunities for more peer interaction outside the company knowing that this often results in greater success in retaining employees.

• **IS THERE A WAY** to involve customers in the company event to make it more of a sales or customer-appreciation event rather than purely about the company?

• **COMPANY EVENTS ARE** a big part of the business world. Their purpose is to build community within the organization. Usually there are one or two each year and often attendance, especially with the Gen Xers, is less than what you wish it were. Is there a way to change them up? Can community be built another way? With only two events each year, the expectations are high and the anticipation of the event builds and the letdown of poor attendance is embarrassing. How about four or five events a year of a much smaller scale? How about something completely different?

CHAPTER TEN

PASSING THE TORCH

Capturing and Transferring Knowledge before It's Too Late

THE NUMBERS PRESENTED at the beginning of this book are rather astounding ... 80 million Boomers, most of whom will likely retire by 2025 and many of whom already have one foot out the door and on the driving range. But along with their workaholic ways and walls adorned with Lucite awards and certificates of recognition, they will be taking something incredibly valuable with them as they head out the door: decades of experience and information.

While their "forever young" spirits may not like to admit it, the Boomers are the elder statesmen of today's business environment. They, along with the handful of Matures who still put in a full day, harbor the skills and the wisdom that is at least partly responsible for bringing most companies to their current positions. Though it is preferable to have the master pass the skills on to the apprentice, skills can always be taught. They are the specific functions that make up the job description, the tasks one manages day-to-day. Skills are often transferrable from job to job and company to company. So if we can't show successors exactly the way it was done before, we can at least assume they will find a way to get it done.

Wisdom, however, is the understanding brought about by time on the job. If skills are the 'how,' wisdom is the 'why' ... and the 'when' and the 'who'. Wisdom is the difference between repeated mistakes and fast-track success. And wisdom can only truly be shared in proximity. It's personal. So companies must have a plan to pass wisdom on before those possessing it retire or embark on new business ventures. With the numbers we've already discussed, it's easy to see why succession planning is critical to long-term success, today more than ever.

Compounding the problem of impending Boomer retirement is the reality that many Xers and Millennials have been leapfrogging through their careers, always chasing the next best opportunity and not necessarily spending enough time in one place to benefit from the company-specific experience of those above (if they were even likely to listen). *The natural transfer of knowledge from one generation to the next over years working side by side is in jeopardy.* How can companies capture the wealth of knowledge locked inside their Boomer (and Mature) leaders and make it available to the next crop of managers and employees – especially if they aren't even "all in" with the company yet? It's a conundrum at the forefront of many leadership boards. If you are to remain viable from generation to generation, then you must find a way for information and insight to change hands.

This is an area that most are still grappling with, though a variety of approaches are being taken by companies around the globe. The proof is still a ways off, since the Boomer retirement is just beginning, but I hope that the stories of some who are taking a stab at harnessing and transferring knowledge can spark a fire that will illuminate a potential best practice for knowledge transfer at your organization.

MAP IT OUT

I SPOKE WITH the VP of talent acquisition at a regional telecom about how her company uses talent mapping to help managers identify potential skill gaps as well as uncover those individuals who are ready now to advance in their careers. This company has a high percentage of Boomers in management positions; however, they happen to be younger Boomers – the average is 48 years old – so they are not facing an imminent retirement swell. As a result, some Boomers are essentially blocking growth and causing a risk that younger employees may move outside the company and take acquired knowledge with them. This company decided to take a long, hard look at who was in senior leadership positions, where there were gaps, and how they might prepare the younger staff to fill those current and future gaps – even if it meant stepping outside traditional career advancement paths. How could they best utilize current talent as well as build strong talent slates for the future?

The answer came in the form of an annual talent review. The talent acquisition team meets with the heads of each function and each division to review each individual's direct reports. They examine employee productivity, promotability and potential, and then place each person in a nine-box grid, a common HR performance and potential matrix. With every employee ranked in the same manner, the company has a road map of the future leaders and knows where to turn when vacancies appear, as well as how to most effectively groom employees for advancement.

Using the nine-box grid, employees who land in the upper right quadrant are strong candidates for promotion, while individuals in the bottom left may be in the wrong job. That doesn't mean they are not worth investment; rather, they will require intervention – either through training or job transfer – to improve their status within the company or at another opportunity. Of course, when budgets constrict, these at-risk employees may also be the easiest to let go. The top left and bottom right boxes indicate employees who could move into the promotable category with some extra guidance. As a result, this tool is also a good way to develop training strategies that meet the development needs of employees, and to offer more tailored instruction to the appropriate employees. As we've discussed, nobody likes to spend time on ineffective or disconnected training.

	Low Performance	Medium Performance	High Performance
High Potential			
Medium Potential			
Low Potential			

At Risk	Good Potential	Promotion Ready

The nine-box grid is an excellent tool for assessing employees; however, it does have pitfalls, the most significant being a lack of common definitions on what each value means. HR managers know that it is critical to have discussions about what makes a good leader – both for today and for tomorrow – so that data is effective in the long run. It is important to make the distinction between business skills and personalities. This specific assessment is about skill; finding the best fit for a personality comes later.

That common definition of leadership can be hard to find when different generations are in the conversation, which makes this step even more important. *Succession planning is about the life of the business, not the personalities within it.* And although solid succession planning creates great road maps for individuals, making it a true win-win for the generations, it is the needs of the company that must come first in order for it to work. To do that, success and leadership abilities must be measured by three things *simultaneously*:

1. A person's output
2. A person's ability to train others
3. A person's readiness to replace themselves if necessary

Yes, all three must be in place, otherwise you may end up facing this same burden again during the next business cycle. Success in leadership is more than just the ability to generate great work; it is the ability to help others do the same. Assessing the staff is only part of the equation. You must also look at the future of your workforce to identify those positions that are at risk – either because the individual in place is facing retirement or promotion, or perhaps because that individual is not a high performer and needs to be relocated to a better career fit.

Eventually, the talent pool and positions need to be prioritized and you can be sure there is a deep bench of talent at each leadership point. If the depth isn't there, you look to the top and middle areas and start grooming them based on a potential vacancy timeline to ensure they will have the necessary business skills in place.

It's worth noting that those highly promotable "top right" employees – those with high performance, high potential – are also at risk, albeit in a different way. Why? Because with their strengths and talent they are significantly more likely to be wooed away by the competition. So you can see that "risky" employees need to be cared for using a broad array of support and incentive mechanisms.

This sounds like basic business management, doesn't it? And it is. There is nothing generationally sacred about talent development, and volumes have been dedicated to this topic alone, so I won't rehash it all. However, the growing need for comprehensive talent management plans is somewhat new and has strong generational influences. There are high numbers of Boomers in leadership positions today, and the manner in which Xers and Millennials have been moving throughout the working world in recent years has made obvious succession paths a thing of the past.

In order to attract younger generations to your company long-term (remember, they simply do not have faith in the lifetime company career) you need to show them how they will be able to grow and have different work experiences with one organization. *Talent management dovetails perfectly with the idea of the meandering career path and the younger generations' need for some level of handholding.* You can identify advancement opportunities that fit the business strengths of the employee and the staffing needs of the company while providing that road map they desire.

"Don't forget to maintain a future orientation in addition to examining the current business environment," the talent manager reminds us. "We are always looking at what will impact our needs – regulations impact technology, technology impacts staffing, etc. In order for talent management to be truly successful, we have to make predictions about the future of the business, not just rely on continuing today's staffing model."

Another client recently embarked on a similar approach, adopting a formal, companywide succession planning model for the first time in its history. When I inquired as to why the time was right to up the ante from the company's previous informal approach, my client shared that recent acquisitions had created a perfect generational storm: With more staff on board from a variety of products and businesses, the family atmosphere where everybody knows everybody was being diluted. As a result it was difficult to pinpoint who the clear successor would be in many situations. The Xers and Millennials were clamoring for direction, and there was no longer a clear path in sight. To solve this problem, they recognized the need for a "full-scale people plan" that would support the company's stated growth strategy.

This organization chose a four-box grid measuring one's degree of performance and specialist skills to evaluate the workforce. The results of the talent assessment are entered into a software program that can map out top talent at any given time, allowing the company to access all promotion-ready staff whenever necessary.

Within three years, this company will have an individual career plan in place for every employee at the management level and up. These plans cover combinations of what a person is capable of and where they would best fit within the organization. Here again, it is imperative that the leadership is willing to reinvent roles so that top talent always has somewhere to land.

EXIT, STAGE LEFT

IF YOU ARE LUCKY enough to have time on your side – with plenty of generational expertise still on the payroll, consider making succession planning part of the formal review process. At a leading international corporation, managers are evaluated on how prepared they are to replace themselves.

At every review, managers are required to share the anticipated training and advancement paths for their direct reports. They must also identify internal candidates for their own positions, as well as those employees' readiness and what is being done to prepare them for this role. The idea, of course, is that the managers themselves will also be advancing through the company ranks, creating the inevitable vacancies. Forward motion is the goal companywide, so there is a premium placed on finding and grooming replacements. However, the company is not blind to the reality that top talent is aggressively scouted by the competition. This "always be prepared" approach covers both scenarios, keeping a constant supply of ready, or near-ready, candidates for all top positions ... and placing that responsibility directly on those who know what qualities the position truly needs.

TAKEAWAYS

Succession planning is increasingly important in a business world where the old master-apprentice cycle is fading away. Without the traditional changing of the guard to rely on, businesses must proactively plan for the growth of employees and provide skill building needed to make sure they have the right people in the right place at the right time.

Questions to ask before you begin:
- What are our most vulnerable and or key positions – both individual people and job descriptions?
- Are we threatened by mass retirements that will require us to transition quite a few people at once?
- Are we ready to embrace succession planning as part of the company culture? If not, how can we get there?

When you are ready to begin assessing talent and mapping out succession strategies there are additional questions to ask of each role:
- What are the competencies of the current job? How were they learned and how long did that take?
- How will the marketplace change in the next three, five and 10 years to impact the needed competencies of this job? What trends are on the horizon, any government regulations pending? Are there areas of the country that tend to lead the industry? Watch them.
- With that in mind, what characteristics will a future candidate need to succeed in this role? Consider both learnable skills and natural/personality traits.
- Is there anyone internally who has a predisposition for this job and its future incarnations?
- Does that person want this job? Never assume.
- Are there similar jobs within or outside your industry where you could find individuals with the required skills?

REEL THEM BACK IN

WHAT IF IT'S TOO LATE? What if your strongest resources have already received their golden watches and are blissfully enjoying retirement. Try bringing them back. Not on the payroll, per se, but as valued advisers. After all, who doesn't like to be viewed as an expert and sought out for his or her wisdom? If you've had a good record of employee satisfaction (and especially if retiree's savings are tied to company stock), retired workers are often eager to talk shop and help their former employers stay successful.

Kellogg Company is headquartered in Battle Creek, Michigan, also known as "Cereal City." Many of the company's employees and retirees live right in town or in nearby Kalamazoo. It is a traditional company town where generations have worked beside each other at the headquarters or production facility for their entire careers. Times are changing and long-timers are long gone. Kellogg recognized that they were facing problems they'd seen before but that few people on staff today had experienced them the first time through. So the company did what any good cereal purveyor would do: They invited folks over for breakfast.

That's right. They issued invitations to local Kellogg retirees, asking them to regular breakfasts with current employees. During these meetings, old-timers and current employees trade stories over a bowl of Special K or Frosted Flakes. There is ample opportunity to ask questions and gain specific advice or insight from individuals who possess decades of company history, who have literally been there and done that. It's not quite the same as working alongside each other for years, but it is a strong step in the right direction.

This is a great example of a company thinking outside the box and discovering ways to connect the company's storytellers with the newcomers, to engage both ends of the generational spectrum and build upon the strengths of each. After all, that's really what we're after – finding ways to connect the generations so that each can have strong footing in the workforce and continue a legacy of productivity despite taking different steps to get there.

TO THINK ON...

• **TOO OFTEN WORKPLACE** leaders are focused exclusively on the day-to-day challenges. They focus on putting out the fires that are burning hottest, brightest, and right on top of them. They don't look to the future and plan for where their business may be headed with the thought of "If I can appropriately prepare for the future, maybe these day-to-day fires won't exist any more." How are you looking ahead? Or are you? How are you exploring trends that may impact your business and how are you preparing to find the talent to exploit those trends?

• **IN YOUR MIND YOU** may see one or two of your employees in key leadership positions in your company in the future. Have you begun preparing them? Are they aware of your vision? Do they want any part of it? You might want to start a conversation with them.

• **WHO ARE YOUR HIGH PERFORMERS?** Are they content or might they be looking for a new challenge on the side? Remember, your stars need to be treated specially – it may be an acknowledgement that they'll be in leadership positions some day or a special pay perk. You run a great risk by ignoring them – they may go to work for your competitor someday if you don't hold on to them.

• **THINK OF YOUR OWN JOB** – what skills does it take to do what you do successfully? If you were to replace yourself, what skill would you want out of the replacement? How about skills you don't have but the job could benefit from? Who do you see who has that special combination?

• **WHERE ARE THE TRENDS** in your industry happening? Are you following them? Is there a parallel industry that might teach you something about where your industry may be going?

• **HOW CAN YOU CONNECT** the future of your company to its history? Whether your business is relatively new or has survived a century of progress, do your employees understand its origins? Do they feel connected to the story as well as the paycheck? Are there individuals — current employees, former employees or retirees — who can share that story, strengthen that connection and build the institutional wisdom base for this generation? How can you bring them together?

PARTING THOUGHTS

OVER THE PAST DOZEN years I have watched companies struggle with how to adapt to the shifting demands and attitudes of their young recruits. Some adapt slowly, almost organically as new minds join the team and thinking evolves to make space for everyone. I've also seen companies mill over the change for some time and then implement drastic changes that shake up their culture and set them on the path to the future. And then there are the companies and managers who put their heads in the sand and hope it all goes away. With the exception of the head-in-the-sand crew, there exists a common thread among the myriad solutions, from industry to industry, private to public: One size does not fit all.

Whatever your solution, be it the ideas brought forth in this book or new strategies that spring from your greater understanding of the generations and your particular workforce, the key to success is flexibility and commitment. *You must believe that these changes are real and therefore be willing to embrace change yourself.* And you must understand that individual satisfaction begets corporate success, and that every individual has different needs. Yes, generational norms and ideals can shed light on these needs, but there will always be nuance and gray areas. What motivates one may bore the next. While a Millennial may appreciate Fridays off, her Gen X counterpart may prefer an earlier start/finish to the day. Flexibility is key.

The companies and managers we've talked about here all embrace the idea of customization within guidelines. They understand that making a business or team run smoothly means keeping your eye on the horizon and adjusting to the currents. Generational differences provide a strong undercurrent to the personal preferences of employees. Whether your company formalizes a policy on flexibility or simply starts looking at how to motivate employees at a personal level, the best practices highlighted in this book demonstrate how looking at individuals and understanding how generational norms may affect their outlooks can result in an engaged workforce that is running at top speed toward your business goals.

As managers and HR professionals continue to explore this topic, we may well find out that the best policy is no policy at all. *In other words, meet every employee where they are and help them get where they and you need to go.* It won't be easy, but it will be effective, worthwhile, and in a new sense, fair. If all else fails, drop anchor, pause, and remember Captain Ted pushing his cargo up the Lower Miss. If he can adjust his well-worn ways and still run a tight ship, so can you.

ENDNOTES

CITATIONS

1   Ted Konnerth. "Hold Onto Your Employees," Electrical Wholesaling 1 Dec. 2008: 89

2   Konnerth.

3   "Today's Graduates Reveal Their Employers of Choice," CNW Group/ Workopolis, Sept. 2008. http://www.newswire.ca/en/releases/archive/september2008/24/c7467.html

4   Louise Esola. "Benefits Management: More Work/Life Programs Cater to Fathers' Needs..." Business Insurance 23 June 2008: 42

5   "A Billion + Change: Why Expand Pro Bono Service and Skills-Based Volunteering," NationalService.gov, http://www.nationalservice.gov/about/initiatives/probono_why.asp

6   Konnerth.

7   "Employee Tenure in 2008" Bureau of Labor Statistics (USDL 08-1344), 26 Sept. 2008

8   Yahoo!hotjobs & Robert Half International "What Millennial Workers Want: How to Attract and Retain Gen Y Employees," 2007

9   Joyce A. Martin, M.P.H.; Brady E. Hamilton, Ph.D.; Paul D. Sutton, Ph.D.;Stephanie J. Ventura, M.A.; Fay Menacker, Dr. P.H.; and Martha L. Munson, M.S.; Division of Vital Statistics "Births: Final Data for 2003" 8 Sept. 2005

10 "Setting the Standard for Corporations Across America," Mitchell Gold+Bob Williams, 2008, http://www.mgbwhome.com/daycare.asp

11 Jen Aronoff. "The Cool Gig at Google" The Charlotte Observer 8 Feb 2009

12 Jessica Marquez. "Retirement Out of Reach..." Workforce Management 1 Nov. 2008:87

13 Catherine Rampell. "Women Now a Majority in American Workplaces," The New York Times 6 Feb. 2010

14 Yahoo!hotjobs & Robert Half International.

15 "Be ingenius" Intuit.com, http://intuitcareers.com/university/new-grads

16 "2007 Best Places to Launch a Career" Business Week http://www.businessweek.com/careers/bplc/2007/1.htm

17 Aronoff.

18 Steven Hendrickson. "Project Boomerang aims to lure Elsewhere Oklahomans," The Edmond Sun 19 Feb. 2009

INTERVIEWS

Clarity. www.clarityny.com

David Zach. www.davidzach.com

EF Education First. www.ef.com

Enterprise Rent-A-Car. www.erac.com

Gold Stars Speakers Bureau. www.goldstars.com

Plante & Moran. www.plantemoran.com

Michael Kitces. www.kitces.com

Midwestern Mechanical. www.mwmech.com

Scott Klososky. www.klososky.com

Strategic Financial Group, L.L.P. www.massmutual.com

ELE

ADDITIONAL REFERENCES

Johanna Ambrosio. "IT is bridging the generation gap, one app at a time," Computerworld 4 March 2009 www.computerworld.com

Karen Corday and Julie Schwartz Weber. "Small Businesses and Work-Family: An Interview with Bruce Philips" Sloan Work and Family Research Network, Boston College, Network News Vol. 10(11) Nov 2008

Paul Greenberg. "Gen X-ers Want More Collaboration With Corporations" CIO Magazine Online 1 March 2006 www.cio.com/article/17907

Matt Guthridge, Emily Lawson and Asmus Komm. "Making talent a strategic priority," The Creative Leadership Forum 16 Jan 2009 www.thecreativeleadershipforum.com

Paula Jacobs. "In the workplace: Tips for managing different generations" IT World 12 Nov 2008 www.itworld.com

Donna Nebenzahl. "Managing the generation gap: Young workers are candid and freer, creating an interesting problem," The Gazette 28 Feb 2009 www.canada.com

Leah Carlson Shepherd. "Keep them at the table: Effective retention strategies depend on the generation," Employee Benefit News, 1 Jul 2008

Michael von Skapinker. "A dose of austerity for a pampered generation" The Financial Times Deutschland, 12 Jan 2008 www.ftd.de

Nick Tasler, Lac D. Su, and Eric Thomas. "The Leadership Vacuum: What we lose with the next generation" Business Lexington 26 December 2008 www.bizlex.com

John A. Warden III and Leland Russell. Winning In Fast Time Venturist Publishing, Sept 2001

Cindy Waxer. "Gen X, Gen Y and Baby Boomers Fight for Same IT Jobs" CIO Magazine Online 16 February 2009: http://www.cio.com/article/481320

Joanne Wojcik. "Benefits Management: Volunteer work benefits employers, employees as well as the community..." Business Insurance 23 June 2008

Daniel Yankelovich. "How Changes in the Economy are Reshaping American Values"

"Questions and Answers about GENERATION X/GENERATION Y: A Sloan Work & Family Research Network Fact Sheet" Sloan Work and Family Research Network, Boston College

"The New Generation: Agents and Their Customers" Best's Review Oct 2008

"Number of Jobs Held, Labor Market Activity and Earnings Growth Among the Youngest Baby Boomers, Results from a Longitudinal Survey" Bureau of Labor Statistics (USDL 08-0860) 27 June 2008